Get Me to the Shrine On Time

Uplifting Tales of the English Countryside

C.H. Merrenby

Copyright © 2025 C.H. Merrenby
Book cover and illustrations copyright © 2025 C.H. Merrenby

C.H. Merrenby asserts the moral right to be identified as the author of this work.

This collection of short stories is entirely a work of fiction. The names, characters and incidents portrayed in it are the work of the author's imagination. Any resemblance to actual persons, living or dead, events or localities is entirely coincidental.

All rights reserved. No part of this publication may be reproduced, stored in a retrieval system, or transmitted, in any form or by any means, electronic, mechanical, photocopying, recording or otherwise, without the prior permission of the author.

First edition 2025

Bible verses are all from the American Standard Version Bible (ASV) which is public domain.

AmDg
and dedicated to the Green-Eyed Gang

Foreword

There are books which must be studied, books which must be shelved and books which must be endured - and then, every once in a while, there are books which are simply to be enjoyed. *This* is one of them.

The author, who knows these green and pleasant fields like one knows the worn handle of a favourite walking stick, has written not to impress the theologians nor to convert the stubborn, but to bring a little comfort to the weary - to provide, in the pages that follow, a sort of literary fireside where the soul may rest its elbows. These stories are neither sermons nor soliloquies, but rather the spiritual equivalent of a warm biscuit offered by a kindly neighbour. They contain Christian themes, yes, but with the light touch of a friend sharing a familiar truth - not the clang of a doctrinal hammer.

In fact, it must be said that this collection will likely be "too Christian" for some, whilst "not Christian enough" for others - "too Catholic" for some and "not Catholic enough" for others. It falls cheerfully between all camps, belonging instead to that nobler, stranger nation: the land of people of good will.

You will find tales both short and long here - some, daringly, even have chapters. They range in mood from the mildly absurd to the mildly profound, but all wear their meaning lightly. As Chesterton once quipped, "Angels can fly because they take themselves lightly," and these stories, too, have wings of that sort.

Accents, it should be said, abound - though not, mercifully, in inconsistent or impenetrable phonetic spellings. The reader is trusted to hear the voices in whatever regional lilt the heart supplies, which is perhaps the most democratic approach to dialect yet devised.

If you are looking for doctrinal clarity or ecclesiastical debate, there are volumes in abundance. But if you are in need of a quiet escape, a laugh, a breath of fresh country air, and maybe - just maybe - a glimpse of grace disguised as a story, then you've come to the right place.

So, close the gate behind you, mind the hens and prepare to meander. There is no rush. The path is soft, the company gentle and the stories quite ready to begin.

Preface

Dear Reader,

You may have noticed that no one has ever said, "I do hope I wake up tomorrow with Type 1 diabetes," or, "What fun it is managing a chronic autoimmune condition!" Quite. Neither have I.

So, if by some extraordinary chance, you happen to be the brilliant mind destined to cure Type 1 diabetes - please, I implore you: put this book down immediately and go and save the world. (This will still be here when you get back - possibly with a sequel.) And on behalf of those who know the carb content of a banana by heart - thank you.

As for everyone else, you may proceed. What lies ahead is gripping stuff - or, at the very least, I hope, pleasantly diverting.

With warmest wishes,

The Author

Contents

Autumn
Get Me to the Shrine on Time	1
The Midnight Garden	6
Three Aunts in a Boat (to Say Nothing of the Nephew)	12
The Parable of the Petal Thief	30
The Pianist at the Wisteria Grand	35

Winter
The Cocoa Hare's Advent Escapade	66
Christmas at Foxglove Hill	76
The Loaf and the Li y	85
The Narrow Way to Lakelore	93
The Pruning of Roses	99

Spring
Panic at the Stables	106
The Garden Meeting	116
The Cove and the Canvas	121
The Return of the Merry Maids	125
Heart of Dartmoor	130

Summer
Petals and Providence	138
The Blue that Wasn't Water	144
The Whiffleton Hall Capers	149
Where the Heather Meets the Sky	163
Lavender Field of Grace	167

Get Me to the Shrine on Time

It was on a particularly foggy Tuesday morning - fog so determined that it seemed to have applied for a permanent residence in the town of Little Widdershins - that Mr Basil Crump found himself standing at the station with nothing but a small leather satchel and an absurdly large sense of urgency. The reason for this urgency, as Mr Crump explained with considerable indignation to the station porter, was that he must reach the Shrine of Saint Aldwyne before precisely eleven o'clock. Not ten fifty-nine, not eleven oh-one - but eleven sharp.

"You see, Mr Porter," he said, jabbing a finger into the mist, "one cannot simply stroll into a shrine like some common tourist. There is a sacred punctuality in these matters. Saint Aldwyne has been waiting centuries. I dare say he's quite particular about the hour."

The porter, who had served in the railway business long enough to have a respectful, if bewildered, patience for eccentrics, raised one bushy eyebrow. "Sir, there's a train at ten-fifteen to Widdershins-on-the-Hill. You'll get there in plenty of time."

"Plenty of time!" Basil echoed, as if the porter had suggested he was late for eternity itself. "Plenty of time is the bane of all saints! I require *exactly* the right time, or the whole ceremony loses its… its… sanctity!"

He clutched his satchel with the desperation of a man who had just remembered he might have left his trousers in the oven at home. The porter, smiling faintly beneath his moustache, shrugged and returned to his duties.

Basil Crump was, by all accounts, a man of curious habits. He had the extraordinary ability to make ordinary events - like catching a train or visiting a shrine - into epic adventures that threatened to dislocate time itself. Yet, for all his fussiness, there was a certain charm in his determined air, as if the universe itself must accommodate his idiosyncrasies.

On the train, Basil found himself in the company of an elderly lady with knitting needles, a young man who read poetry aloud as though the words might vanish if unspoken, and a small, remarkably intelligent terrier named Pippin. Basil nodded at Pippin as if the dog were an old friend from seminary school. "We must keep our wits about us," he whispered to the terrier. "Time is a tyrant today."

The journey, which ought to have been uneventful, quickly became a theatre of absurdity. At every stop, Basil fretted over the exact alignment of the minute-hand on his watch with the sacred hour. When the train slowed at a particularly picturesque bridge, he sprang from his seat, demanding that the ticket collector confirm the precise time to the second. The ticket collector, a man of uncommon patience, but little sense, consulted his pocket watch and replied, "Ten forty-five and a half, sir."

"Half!" Basil groaned. "Half is no part of the hour. Half is the shadow of eternity! We are lost, lost to punctuality!"

By the time the train finally arrived at Widdershins-on-the-Hill, Basil was so flustered that he nearly ran straight into a milk cart. The milkman, accustomed to the eccentricities of visitors to this sleepy town, merely shook his head. "Saint Aldwyne's shrine, is it?" he said knowingly. "Better make haste, then, or the saint will be cross."

Basil, clutching his satchel as though it contained the Holy Grail itself, hurried up the hill, Pippin trotting obediently at his heels. The path wound steeply through orchards and over cobblestones and, with each step, Basil's anxiety grew. He imagined Saint Aldwyne tapping his celestial foot, glancing at the invisible clock, and murmuring, *'Where is that Crump fellow? Always late, that one."*

Halfway up the hill, Basil encountered a young boy balancing a basket of apples. "Excuse me, my good fellow," Basil panted, "can you tell me the time?"

The boy looked at him in bemusement. "It's ten fifty-five, sir. But… you look like you're running from the devil himself."

"I am running from *something infinitely worse*," Basil corrected. "I am running from irreverence and temporal negligence!"

By now, Pippin had taken it upon himself to bark at a passing chicken, causing Basil to trip over a particularly insistent root. He landed in a pile of fallen leaves, his hat spinning into a puddle, and his satchel opened just enough to release a small cloud of neatly folded notes and one very important missal. He scrambled to gather them, muttering, "Order must be preserved… sacred order… oh, woe!"

At last, panting and slightly muddied, Basil reached the shrine. The bell began to toll eleven. A hush fell over the small gathering of pilgrims and curious townsfolk. Basil straightened his jacket, wiped his shoes on the edge of the steps, and strode forward with the dignity of a man who had conquered time itself.

Inside the shrine, a small, ornate altar awaited him. Candles flickered, and the air smelled faintly of incense and apple pie - a curious combination that only seemed appropriate to the eccentric charm of Widdershins-on-the-Hill. Basil knelt, opening his missal with deliberate reverence. Pippin curled at his feet, occasionally glancing up as if to ensure that the saint did not take offence at the dog's presence.

And then, on the eleventh strike of eleven o'clock, something remarkable happened. A gust of wind blew through the shrine, scattering a few candles, but leaving Basil's missal untouched. A single beam of sunlight fell upon the altar, illuminating the golden figure of Saint Aldwyne in such a way that it seemed to nod approvingly at Basil.

Basil, overwhelmed with emotion, whispered, "I have arrived on time, dear saint. I have kept the hour. I have -"

A small cough interrupted him. Basil turned to see a man in a brown cloak, peering from behind a column. "Ah, you must be Mr Crump," the man said. "I'm the shrine's caretaker. It's rare to see someone so... exact."

Basil stood, brushing dust from his jacket. "Exactitude is not merely rare - it is the very essence of devotion," he replied solemnly.

The caretaker nodded. "Well, devotion aside, you might like to know... Mass usually starts at ten."

For a moment, Basil's face betrayed the tiniest flicker of horror. Then he laughed - a laugh so full and rich that it echoed through the shrine and startled Pippin into a discreet growl.

"Ah! So the saint is patient after all," Basil said, bowing deeply to the altar. "Patience, like humour, is a virtue in which I am… temporarily deficient!"

The caretaker smiled. "You've brought charm to the shrine, Mr Crump. That counts for something."

And, indeed, it did. Basil spent the rest of the morning at the shrine, chatting with pilgrims, recounting tales of his temporal trials, and generally delighting the townsfolk with his unflagging enthusiasm. By the time he left, Pippin trotting beside him and the sun high in the sky, Basil felt that he had accomplished not only punctuality, but something infinitely more important: the spreading of cheer and gentle absurdity in a world that often took itself far too seriously.

As he descended the hill, Basil paused and looked back at the shrine. "Farewell, Saint Aldwyne," he whispered. "May all who come after me find a half-minute of grace and a full measure of laughter."

And somewhere, it seemed, the saint nodded in agreement, perhaps slightly amused at the human insistence that even divine matters should be governed by a precise timetable.

Basil Crump, satisfied with the morning's adventure, strode towards the station with Pippin at his side, already plotting how he might one day return - on time, of course - but prepared, as always, for the delightful chaos of life's little interruptions.

The Midnight Garden

It was a crisp late-autumn evening when Amanda, Eric and Kateri snuggled down beneath a patchwork of quilts in the little upstairs room of their grandparents' cottage. The air smelt faintly of woodsmoke and lavender sachets and from somewhere down the narrow hallway, the soft chime of the old grandfather clock marked the hour.

The three children should have been asleep. But sleep, like a shy cat, had slipped away. There was something magical in the air tonight - something that shimmered just beyond the edge of knowing.

Outside, the countryside had grown dusky and still. It was the sort of night where the stars come close enough to whisper secrets and the wind carries stories through the hedgerows. The garden lay silent beyond the frosted windows, but there was a glow - a soft, flickering glow - that hadn't been there before.

Then came a quiet knock on the bedroom door.

"Come along, little ones," whispered Grandma, peeking her head in. Her grey hair was tucked beneath a woollen hat and Grandad stood behind her, holding up three woollen jumpers and a set of wellies apiece. "We've something to show you."

The children sat up, wide-eyed.

"At this hour?" gasped Amanda.

"But it's bedtime," said Kateri, though she was already pushing back the covers.

Grandad chuckled. "It is - but sometimes the best surprises come when you least expect them."

They bundled into the warm knitted jumpers, their wellies clomping softly down the stairs. Grandma handed each of them a lantern and together they stepped out into the chilly night.

The garden stretched before them like something from a dream.

Winding paths had been lit with tiny lanterns, each one glowing golden among the fallen leaves. Arched bowers of ivy and briar were woven with fairy lights and from every tree branch hung glass jars catching the light like jewels. The children gasped as they stepped into the wonder of it.

"It's like Narnia," whispered Eric.

"It's like Heaven," said Amanda.

Kateri clutched her lantern. "It's all lit up… like a secret place waiting to be found."

"'Thy word is a lamp unto my feet, and light unto my path,'" murmured Grandma, smiling. "Psalm one hundred and nineteen."

The children followed the lantern-lit trail, their breath turning to silver in the cold air. Every corner revealed something new - wooden stepping stones edged with moss, a hidden bench beneath a tree glowing with twinkling stars and even a swing that creaked gently in the breeze.

Finally, the path opened into a glade that none of them had ever seen before.

At its centre was a round wooden table, laid out beneath a canopy of golden fairy lights. Around it stood five chairs, each with a tartan blanket draped over the back. The table itself was bedecked with glowing lanterns and a cake stand topped with slices of chocolate and orange cake. A thermos of warm apple juice steamed gently in the cool air.

"Oh…" breathed Kateri.

"This is a midnight feast," Eric said, reverently.

"It's beautiful," whispered Amanda.

They sat down with Grandma and Grandad, wrapped in blankets, and ate cake in the middle of the midnight garden. The only sounds were the rustling of the wind, the far-off hoot of an owl and the occasional delighted giggle.

After the cake had been eaten - every crumb - and the warm apple juice had filled them with a cosy glow, the children slipped from their chairs, lanterns swinging from mittened hands.

"Let's explore," said Amanda, her eyes bright.

"Let's *run*," said Eric, already darting down one of the winding paths.

They ran - laughing, breath clouding in the cold - as golden lamplight spilled across the dark earth. Their boots thudded softly on the grass, kicking up curls of frost like silvery mist.

The garden, in the hush of late October, had become a realm all its own: neither fully of this world, nor yet a dream.

They played hide-and-seek between the ivy-wrapped arbours and chased one another through narrow hedged corridors that twisted and turned like old stories. The lanterns above bobbed gently in the branches, some steady, others flickering - as though the stars themselves had come down to join in their joy.

In a quiet corner they found a forgotten birdbath, rimmed with frost and filled with leaves, like a fairy's wishing pool. Kateri leaned over it and whispered a hope into the water. What she wished, no one asked. But something in her smile said it would stay with her forever.

Eric discovered a circle of toadstools nestled beneath a hazel tree and they all stood solemnly around it, wondering if they'd stumbled upon the very edge of an elfin glade. The air here was still, but tingled as if it held its breath.

All the while, Grandma and Grandad watched from the path, hands clasped. Their faces were lit with quiet gladness - not just for the garden or even the feast - but for the children themselves, who were, in that moment, fully alive with wonder. It was enough.

And then - just as the final lantern flickered and the last swing of laughter drifted into the trees - the wind changed. It came gentler now, like a lullaby.

Hand in hand, they made the walk back to the cottage through the glowing paths. The lanterns, which had shone so boldly at the start, now dimmed slowly behind them, like theatre lights after the final bow.

At the back step, Eric looked up at Grandad. "Did you build all this just for us?"

Grandad didn't answer right away. He knelt instead, brushing frost from the toes of Eric's boots. "Sometimes," he said quietly, "love looks like lanterns in the dark."

They slipped off their wellies at the door, carried their lanterns upstairs and climbed beneath the patchwork quilts without a word.

Outside, the garden rested once more in silence. But something had changed. For in that garden, a memory had been planted - glowing gently like firelight - and would bloom in each of their hearts forever.

Kateri turned in bed, her breath slowing.

"I think," she whispered into the stillness, "that might have been the best night of my life."

Amanda smiled, eyes closed. "Do you think it really happened?"

"Of course it did," said Eric, but his voice was already slipping into sleep.

If Grandma and Grandad had peeked into the room just then, they would have found three little children sleeping soundly under quilts of stitched stars - faces turned toward dreams where golden lanterns still swayed in the trees.

As the beloved grandparents closed the cottage curtains

and turned out the last light, they looked once more toward the darkened garden. It had returned to quiet now. But in their hearts, they knew:

Something holy had passed through the night. Not loud. Not grand. But golden. Gentle. And eternal.

'In him was life; and the life was the light of men. And the light shineth in the darkness; and the darkness apprehended it not.' - John 1:4-5

'Every good gift and every perfect gift is from above, coming down from the Father of lights" - James 1:17

Three Aunts in a Boat (to Say Nothing of the Nephew)

A cheerful tale of slow travel, warm tea and steady grace along the canal

Chapter One: In Which Not Much Happens, Except Everything That Matters

Providence moved like an old hymn - slow, steady and entirely unbothered by the modern world. It glided along the Kennet and Avon Canal under trees that had turned the colour of well-baked crumble topping, scattering leaves across the water like notes on a page of music. She was a traditional narrowboat, painted in rich green with cream and red detailing and her cabin sides were decorated with hand-painted roses and castles - old canal art that turned every curve and corner into something cheerfully splendid. A red Buckby-style can sat by the hatch and *Providence's* brass tiller caught the light like a wink from an old friend.

At the stern stood Aunty Ava, alert at the tiller, her wool coat buttoned to the chin and her gloves leather, lined and entirely unsuited to tea-pouring, which is why she didn't attempt it.

Aunty Teresa emerged from the cabin with a tray bearing four mugs of Yorkshire tea, two slices of ginger loaf and a selection of biscuits. She looked over the water with a sigh of contentment.

"If I were in charge," she said, "everyone would be required to spend at least three days on a canal boat each year. We'd have fewer complaints and far better manners."

"Some of us would just spill more tea," said Mark, catching his mug as the boat nudged the bank with the gentlest of bumps.

At twelve, Mark was equal parts curiosity and commentary, with wind-ruffled hair and the composed manners of a boy being brought up by three aunts who considered etiquette only slightly less important than oxygen.

"Character-building," said Aunty Felicity, pulling a blanket around her shoulders and balancing her mug on her knee. "It teaches you to adapt. Life, like tea, is best approached with steadiness and a firm saucer."

"No saucers on this boat," Aunty Ava called back. "We've enough to wash without adding delicate crockery to the rota."

"We're travelling at walking pace," said Aunty Felicity, sipping. "We have time to hand-wash the entire contents of John Lewis, if needed."

Mark, who had appointed himself Official Spotter of Wildlife and Unusual Objects, peered through a pair of antique binoculars that had previously belonged to a great uncle with a passion for birdwatching and small, impractical gadgets.

"There's a heron up ahead," he announced. "It's doing that thing where it pretends not to be interested in us, but really it's watching every crumb we drop."

"It's a heron, not a burglar," said Aunty Teresa. "Though I suppose you can't trust anything with knees that bend backwards."

Mark lowered the binoculars. "I think it looks wise."

"Everything looks wise when it's standing still," said Aunty Ava. "It's only once they start flapping that you see their true character. Same as people, really."

They passed under a stone bridge with ivy trailing from the arch like old lace. A man on the towpath lifted a hand in greeting; Aunty Ava nodded solemnly in return.

"He looked friendly," said Mark.

"People usually are on the towpath," Aunty Teresa replied. "I think the canal brings it out in them. You can't rush here. You can't shout. It'd be like shouting in a library."

"Or a greenhouse," Aunty Felicity added.

"Or a cathedral," said Mark, after a pause.

Aunty Teresa smiled. "Exactly."

There was a brief, companionable silence as the boat drifted on. Then Aunty Ava said, "I rather liked St John's in Bath. Nice to be able to moor up and just walk to Mass without any fuss."

"Oh, and the walk up to the church through the city," Aunty Felicity added, dreamily. "Those Georgian buildings - I never tire of them. That honey-coloured stone looks like a jar of thick-set local honey. Makes me want to dip in a big spoon."

Aunty Ava gave a small sigh. "You could romanticise a

paving slab if it reminded you of something sweet."

After the bridge, they moored briefly near a hedgerow heavy with late blackberries. Mark was dispatched with a tub and came back with six berries, one leaf and a good number of scratches.

"You picked the ones the birds rejected," Aunty Felicity observed.

"Let's call it a symbolic harvest," said Aunty Teresa. "We'll eat them with dignity and far too much cream."

Back on the move, the sky turned a soft pewter and a few leaves began to fall in earnest. Inside the cabin, a small kettle puffed gently on the stove, while the warmth from the fire turned the narrow boat into a snug little ark, carrying four people, several woollen blankets and half a ginger cake over the Dundas Aqueduct.

As they floated along the aqueduct, high above the Avon valley, the faintest of mists weaving over the river and the old school boathouse below, a sudden sound split the stillness - a deep, exultant whoosh. The Royal Scot steam engine roared into view on the track beneath, a streak of smoke and steel that vanished almost as quickly as it came. It was gone in the blink of an eye, but left behind a jolt of wonder - a fleeting marvel sewn into their journey like a brass button on a wool coat: unnecessary, but utterly splendid.

"Good gracious alive!" said Aunty Teresa, clutching her tea. "Was that a train down there or the entire Industrial Revolution in a hurry?"

"Looked like it was late for a very important century," said Mark, still peering after it.

"What a glorious interruption!" declared Aunty Felicity, eyes bright. "I saw that engine once at Rugby station when I was small. Thought it was the most magnificent thing on Earth. Still might be."

Aunty Ava gave a rare smile. "And now it's come back to give you a second opinion."

They all watched the valley for a moment longer, listening to the echo fade into the hills.

Then, as if nothing had happened, the kettle inside let out a soft hiss, a moorhen darted across the canal ahead and *Providence* slipped forward once more - slow, steady and entirely unbothered by the excitement of passing time and steam locomotives.

Then, as the boat drifted into a slow, sweeping bend, the aqueduct fell away behind them and the valley melted from sight, replaced by a parade of autumn splendour - trees and shrubs crowding the towpath in vivid shades of ochre, flame and wine-red, their branches arching overhead like a slow-burning awning, heavy with the quiet majesty of the season. The boat gently rocked as Aunty Ava adjusted their course.

"I do think people underestimate how good it is for the soul to go slowly," said Aunty Teresa, handing out fresh mugs.

"It forces you to notice things," Aunty Ava agreed. "Like that duck that's been tailing us for the last half-mile. I think it's after your biscuit."

"It's not the only one," said Mark, pocketing the remaining piece defensively.

"Let it be a lesson," said Aunty Felicity. "When you share your journey, someone will always want your biscuit."

Mark leaned on the rail beside her.

"Do you think we'll get where we're going?" he asked.

"That depends," she said, eyes forward.

"On what?"

"On whether we remember that the point is to travel, not just to arrive."

He frowned, considering it.

"Is that one of those sayings that sounds clever now and confusing later?"

"It's one of those sayings that'll make perfect sense next year."

Later, after they'd moored for the night beneath a canopy of rustling trees, and the sun had dipped behind the hedgerows, the four of them sat wrapped in blankets, squashed up together on the stern deck. The water was glass-still. Not a ripple stirred except from the faintest nudge of a passing swan. There were no engines, no rush, no horns. Just a kettle whistling quietly in the cabin and the gentle creak of the ropes.

Then the moon rose - a great, glowing harvest moon, low and impossibly large, as if it had drifted a little closer to listen in. It hung in the sky like a lantern made of pearl and fire, lighting the canal with a light so soft it felt like being touched. The trees were edged with silver, the water turned to liquid gold and even their breath seemed to shimmer in the stillness.

No one said a word. They simply watched as the moon held its place above the world, quiet and magnificent - a reminder that some things are best admired in silence. In their hearts, prayers of hope, thanks and praise rose up, as simple and pure as the moon itself.

Mark leaned back and sighed. "I think this might be better than any holiday I've ever had."

"It's not a holiday," said Aunty Teresa. "It's a retreat."

Aunty Ava nodded. "A journey."

Aunty Felicity smiled. "A floating tea room."

As Mark looked up into the night sky, his eyes lingered on the bright moon.

"It's all of it, isn't it?"

They all agreed.

Moral of the Story

When you travel slowly and pay attention, you find more than peace - you find perspective. And when your companions are kind and the tea is strong, the journey becomes its own reward.

Chapter Two: Beethoven, Biscuits and the Swing Bridge of Confusion

The morning mist curled across the canal like steam from a heavenly teapot. It clung to the reeds, softened the trees and turned the narrowboat *Providence* into a floating silhouette, gently bobbing in its mooring like it wasn't entirely sure about the day yet.

Inside, Aunty Teresa stirred porridge with the dedication of someone who believed breakfast should be both nourishing and slightly overcooked. A faint hymn hummed from the radio - something in E flat, muffled by the saucepan lid.

"Has anyone seen my gloves?" called Aunty Ava, into the cabin.

"They're on the shelf next to the marmalade," Aunty Felicity replied from the bow. "You took them off to butter a scone."

"Ah," said Aunty Ava, as if that explained everything.

By mid-morning, as they set off, the mist began to lift in gentle folds, revealing the landscape in slow-motion. Trees along the towpath emerged like polite spectators. A single cow blinked at them through a hedge, then returned to chewing with meditative calm.

Mark spotted it and pointed. "That cow has seen things."

"Cows always look like they've read the Book of Ecclesiastes," said Aunty Teresa. "All is vanity, and the grass is damp."

They rounded a bend and saw it: the swing bridge. The great equaliser of boating holidays. It looked innocent enough - just a modest little iron gate stretched over the canal like it was taking a nap - but every boater knew this was where tempers and tillers alike were tested.

"Manual or electric?" asked Aunty Felicity warily.

Aunty Ava narrowed her eyes. "Manual. There's a sign."

"Which means?" Mark asked, already reaching for the windlass.

"It means we do the work," said Aunty Teresa. "And try not to look smug when we succeed."

They moored temporarily by the bridge landing. Mark jumped off, windlass in hand. Aunty Felicity followed with a biscuit tin for moral support.

"Right," said Aunty Ava. "Gate key in, lock open, wind to release."

Mark did his best, turning the stubborn gear with the intensity of a twelve-year-old boy defusing a bomb in a spy film.

"It's jammed," he said after thirty seconds.

"You said that at the last one," Aunty Teresa reminded him, "and it turned out you were standing on the hinge."

"This time it's *really* jammed."

"Let me have a look," said a voice from the towpath.

A man in a long green coat and a hat shaped like a teapot stepped forward. Behind him trotted a small, rather pleased-looking goat.

"Good morning," said Aunty Teresa brightly.

"Alan Birkett," said the man. "Retired bellringer. Still got both ears. This is Beethoven."

The goat gave a brief nod, as though proud of the introduction.

"Beethoven?" asked Mark. "Is he musical?"

"He only reacts to organ music," said Alan. "Can't stand pop. He's very particular."

"I like him already," said Aunty Ava, inspecting the swing bridge.

"I'll give you a hand," said Alan, producing a second windlass from his coat pocket, as if he kept spares for canal emergencies.

Between them, and with some firm persuasion (and one off-key bleat from Beethoven), the bridge eventually swung open with the majestic reluctance of an Elizabethan drawbridge. *Providence* crept through, obedient and unflustered.

"Much obliged," said Aunty Ava, steering through.

"Anytime," Alan called. "If you're heading up as far as Bradford-upon-Avon, stop in at St Mary's Lock. My wife's just made a fresh batch of parkin, toffee apples and bonfire toffee - proper autumn fare, none of your shop-bought nonsense."

Aunty Felicity waved enthusiastically. "We never say no to seasonal bribery."

"And keep an eye on the riverbank past the next bend," Alan added. "I spotted a family of otters there two mornings ago - quiet as anything, tucked in among the reeds."

"Otters!" Mark perked up immediately, already reaching for his binoculars.

"Add that to today's agenda," said Aunty Ava, adjusting the tiller. "Parkin, parley and potential otter sightings."

"Best kind of schedule," Aunty Teresa called back, as the boat drifted on, the gentle slosh of the water mingling with the distant bleat of Beethoven and the promise of something quietly marvellous around the next curve.

Later, tied up along a wide stretch of canal near a hedge full of blackbirds, the four travellers settled with tea and the last of the ginger cake. The mist had fully lifted now, revealing the countryside in full autumn splendour: russet fields, scattered leaves and the soft clop of a horse in a nearby lane.

Mark lay on the roof of the boat, arms behind his head.

"Even though we didn't see any otters, that was a good day," he said.

"We've only had the morning," Aunty Teresa pointed out.

"Well, I've already earned my tea. And made a goat friend."

Aunty Ava passed him a mug. "Small victories are still victories."

"I think Beethoven should join the crew," said Aunty Felicity. "He's reliable and he doesn't argue about where to moor."

"I argue for the sake of lively debate," said Aunty Teresa.

"You argue because you like choosing where the kettle goes."

"And what hymn we listen to after lunch."

Mark closed his eyes, grinning. "I vote we form a permanent boat crew and do this every autumn."

Aunty Ava gave him a long look. "If you keep improving at windlass work and biscuit preservation, we'll consider it."

"I'd like us to go on a *steam engine holiday* too," murmured Aunty Felicity, dreamily. "If there *is* such a thing…"

As the autumn afternoon stretched on, the rich scent of jacket potatoes filled the air, mingling with the crisp, earthy aroma of the season. The sun, dipping low, cast long shadows on the water, turning the surface into a shimmering mirror that seemed to stretch forever.

That evening, once safely moored, three aunts and a nephew lost themselves in a whirlwind of card games, the air alive with laughter and light-hearted banter around the table in the saloon. The world outside seemed to vanish entirely, as if they had slipped into a moment where only the warmth, laughter and soft glow of the cabin existed. The only reminder of reality came now and then, when a passing boat sent a gentle ripple through the water, making *Providence* sway ever so slightly - like a quiet, contented dance in the dark.

Ducks drifted by, heading home to bed, their movements serene and unhurried. The canal lay still, as though holding its breath, embracing them all in a peaceful hush.

Moral of the Story

Even in the small misadventures - the jammed bridge, the lost gloves, the unexpected goat - we find God's quiet grace. When life moves slowly, peace finds us. And sometimes, it wears a bell.

Chapter Three: Of Buttered Bath Buns and the Sheep with Opinions

The dawn came in quietly, as if it didn't want to wake anyone unnecessarily. Mist rose from the water in soft curls, like breath from a steaming cup, and the canal looked for all the world like a silver ribbon laid gently across the land.

Aboard *Providence*, all was still - until the kettle began to mutter.

Aunty Ava was the first to rise, as always. She preferred the morning, especially when it arrived respectfully and not with alarms. She stood at the stern with her tea, wrapped in her wool coat and the satisfaction of being up before everyone else.

Mark emerged next, blinking like a creature who hadn't fully agreed to being awake.

"I had a dream the boat grew wheels and drove off across a field."

"That's not a dream," said Aunty Ava, "that's an insurance headache."

Aunty Teresa appeared from below, holding a pair of thick woollen socks and wearing an expression that suggested she'd just remembered something mildly glorious.

"It's the perfect day for a picnic," she declared.

"In the mist?" asked Aunty Felicity, now making toast.

"Yes," said Aunty Teresa firmly. "Picnics aren't about weather. They're about optimism with sandwiches."

"We've had worse ideas," said Aunty Ava, sipping her tea. "Remember the time we picnicked on that beach with the tide timetable written in Latin?"

"That was character-building," said Aunty Teresa.

"It was cold," said Aunty Felicity. "And damp."

"And educational," Aunty Teresa insisted.

By late morning, the mist had mostly lifted and the boat moved gently along the canal. The hedgerows dripped with dew. Trees on both sides wore their best patchwork of gold and crimson, and the water was so still it seemed more mirror than canal.

Mark was steering with exaggerated focus. "Tell me again how I know if I'm going straight?"

"If you're not hitting anything, assume the best," said Aunty Ava.

Aunty Teresa was spreading butter and jam onto Bath buns inside the cabin. "If anyone sees a bench or patch of grass with fewer than five angry geese, that's where we stop."

Aunty Felicity popped her head out. "What if there are sheep?"

"Only if they look contemplative."

They found a perfect spot shortly after a gentle bend - an open meadow just beside the towpath, where the grass was soft and the only sound was the slow flap of crows overhead.

Mark unpacked the rug. Aunty Teresa laid out the Bath buns and cheese. Aunty Felicity poured flask-tea like a woman conducting a ceremony.

Then came the sheep.

A single one at first - white, wide and waddling toward them with the conviction of a professional.

"She looks like she has opinions," Mark said.

"She looks like she's about to *join* the picnic," said Aunty Teresa.

"Don't be ridiculous," said Aunty Ava, just as the sheep settled herself beside the edge of the blanket with the ease of someone finding their usual pew.

"I think she's family now," said Mark, offering her a crust of Bath bun. She sniffed, considered and declined.

"She's judging the cheese," Aunty Teresa muttered. "I can feel it."

They ate amid the company of sheep and crows, all of whom stared as if personally offended by every bite.

"It's hard to be grateful under surveillance," said Aunty Felicity.

"They're just curious," said Aunty Ava. "Possibly philosophical."

"They've clearly never seen a Bath bun before," said Mark.

He paused and looked across the field. "Do you think God made sheep so we'd learn not to take ourselves too seriously?"

"Possibly," said Aunty Teresa, "but only if He made goats so we'd learn humility."

Aunty Ava raised an eyebrow. "And chickens?"

"Discipline," said Aunty Felicity without hesitation.

On the way back to the boat, Mark carried the picnic bag and the profound sense of having been deeply misunderstood by livestock.

"I don't think she liked me," he said.

"She didn't know how to place you," said Aunty Teresa. "You weren't carrying food and you didn't look like a shepherd."

"Could've been worse," said Aunty Ava. "She might've followed us back."

At which point, of course, she did.

For ten full minutes, the ewe followed them along the towpath, stopping when they stopped, walking when they walked and pausing at the mooring with a look of mild disappointment when they boarded the boat without her.

"Leave her," said Aunty Ava gently. "This is not the season for acquiring sheep."

"She looks like she has things to say," Mark protested.

"Sheep always do," said Aunty Teresa. "But you rarely get to the bottom of it."

That evening, as the fire crackled in the tiny stove and the canal turned golden under the falling light, they sat once again inside *Providence's* cosy saloon, peacefully slurping hot chocolate. Stretching out his hand, Mark drew back the curtains slightly so he could look out toward the darkening horizon.

"Do you think she'll remember us?"

"The sheep?" asked Aunty Felicity.

"Yes."

"Oh, definitely," said Aunty Teresa. "We made an impression."

"She's probably telling the others," said Aunty Ava. "About the four strange people with Bath buns and belligerent Brie."

"And one very fine picnic," said Aunty Felicity, lifting her mug in salute.

Another glorious day of their holiday drew to its happy close and, day by day, as always, *Providence* did what she did best - carried them gently forward, together.

Moral of the Story

Sometimes God sends silence. Sometimes He sends sheep. Either way, peace arrives - if you've got a blanket, some tea and the grace to laugh gently at yourself.

The Parable of the Petal Thief

I. The Village That Bloomed with Secrets

There are villages in England that have grown like mushrooms - unplanned, unpoetic and unnervingly near train stations. But Fallowbrook-in-the-Vale was not one of these.

Fallowbrook was the kind of village that only appeared in watercolour or prayer. It was tucked like a forget-me-not among the mossy hills of Shropshire, where even the fog had good manners and the sheep looked vaguely Anglican.

Its cottages were made of stone so old and so moss-covered that people had long ceased to distinguish between house and hill. And its people, though they went to Mass out of habit rather than heresy, still bowed their heads when the bells rang - more from reverence than rheumatism.

But what gave Fallowbrook its peculiar glory - its grand, golden distinction - was the Annual Chrysanthemum Society Show, a competitive flower festival with more tension than a diocesan budget meeting and more colour than a high Anglo-Catholic vestment drawer.

The chrysanthemums were judged not only by size and bloom, but also by things like "temperament," "ethical composure," and - most controversially - "spiritual optimism." One judge once attempted to explain what that meant and was never asked back.

II. The Man with the Scarf and the Theology of Gardening

Our hero, if we must stoop to such vulgar taxonomy, was Mr Eustace Nudge - a short, roundish man of theological tendencies and no known profession. He had an ill-advised beard that suggested he'd once tried to look serious and failed. He always wore a scarf, even in July, and claimed it was for reasons of doctrine, not draught.

Eustace had once begun a book on "The Divine Imprudence of Bees," which no one had asked for and even fewer had read. But he had the peculiar gift of irritating the self-righteous and comforting the guilty, and so had become, in some unofficial capacity, the village's philosopher, fool and friend.

He lived alone in a sloping cottage that contained one rickety chair, twelve cracked teacups and fourteen copies of *The Everlasting Man* with different underlinings.

And every year, without fail, Eustace entered the Chrysanthemum Show with a small, slightly crooked bloom named 'Judith,' which never won, never impressed and never once stopped growing.

III.   The Scandal in the Marquee

The scandal broke - if that is the correct word for something so entirely floral - on the morning of judging.

Lady Evergrace, doyenne of the local aristocracy and undefeated champion of the Chrysanthemum Show, had arrived early to spritz her entry, a crimson colossus named "Martyrdom of St Cecilia." She screamed. Loudly.

"Someone," she declared, "has **snipped off three petals!**"

The village reeled.

A crime against chrysanthemums was not merely horticultural; it was practically blasphemy. For, in Fallowbrook, flowers were not only symbols of beauty - they were *moral metaphors*. To tamper with a bloom was to tamper with truth itself.

Suspicion fell, of course, on Eustace Nudge.

He was always at the Show. He was always muttering things about humility and the hidden virtues of small plants. And worst of all, he had once said (and repeated) that, "no one should win every year unless they were the Holy Ghost."

By noon, a committee had been formed. By one, it had resigned. By two, Eustace was brought before the Chrysanthemum Society Tribunal (which met behind the tea tent).

IV. The Trial of the Twisted Theology

Eustace stood, scarf crooked, eyes twinkling, before a row of elderly women with more pins in their hats than in a seamstress's drawer.

"Mr Nudge," began the Chairwoman, Mrs Parsnip, "you have been observed loitering near Lady Evergrace's marquee. You have made *remarks*. And you have submitted, once again, a flower that appears to be in a state of repentance."

"It leans slightly," said Eustace. "That's not repentance. That's realism."

"Did you or did you not pluck petals from Lady Evergrace's chrysanthemum?"

"No," said Eustace.

The crowd murmured. A young curate fainted from the suspense (or possibly the heat).

"I should not," Eustace went on, "pluck the petals of any bloom - though I am convinced that some of them have far too many. But may I say something... unwise?"

He was given a stern nod.

"I think," said Eustace slowly, "that it is possible to win so many times, that one forgets what it means to **grow**."

A gasp.

He went on, his eyes soft. "The Christian life is not a matter of perfection, but perseverance. Not winning, but blooming again after the frost. I bring 'Judith' every year not because she wins - she never does - but because she grows. Not in a hothouse. Not with special lamps. Just here. In soil. Under sun and rain. A flower like that can remind us that grace is not always grand, and beauty is not always bold."

The silence was thick as clotted cream.

And then, slowly - *one by one* - the crowd began to clap.

Even Lady Evergrace, whose petals had been pinched, dabbed her eyes and muttered, "Oh dash it, he's right."

V. The Petal Thief Confesses

It was Mrs Parsnip's corgi, as it turned out, who had entered the marquee and - acting on pure instinct or refined taste - nibbled at the St Cecilia bloom.

A floral tragedy, yes. A theological one? Perhaps not.

Lady Evergrace declared herself relieved that it had not been a case of sabotage by Jesuits. Eustace offered the corgi a biscuit and was elected "Honorary Non-Competitor for Life."

As for 'Judith', she was given a "Special Commendation for Moral Encouragement" and Eustace declared it the first rational award the Society had ever bestowed.

VI. The Meaning of Chrysanthemums

On the following Sunday, Eustace was seen planting three new chrysanthemum bulbs near the churchyard wall.

A boy passing by asked him why he bothered.

"They probably won't bloom 'til next year," he said.

Eustace smiled. "That's why I plant them."

And as the bells began to toll, calling the faithful and the doubting alike into a crooked little Catholic church, the village of Fallowbrook-in-the-Vale turned, once again, toward Heaven - among chrysanthemums and laughter and grace.

The Pianist at the Wisteria Grand

2nd September

Dear Diary,

Today I tried to be holy. I really did.

I woke up at 6:45am (which, if you're me, is practically canonisation material), lit my Lourdes candle, and said Morning Prayer with the best of intentions. I imagined myself floating through the day serenely, like one of those radiant saints in stained-glass windows.

Then I stubbed my toe on the laundry basket. Which, frankly, is exactly the sort of thing that happens the moment you decide you're going to be virtuous.

Anyway.

By 10am, I was at *The Wisteria Grand Hotel*, where I play the piano - mostly for afternoon teas, but also for dinners, weddings, the odd gala evening… basically whenever they want background music and can't afford a string quartet. Picture it: acres of New Forest woodland stretching away outside, ancient oak trees already dropping crisp golden leaves, ponies ambling across the verges as though they own the place (which, to be fair, they do). Then there's the grand gravel drive sweeping up to the hotel, and this enormous white-stone building with pillars and too many windows to count. It's the sort of place where you expect to bump into Jane Austen and a film crew hiding behind the topiary.

The Wisteria Grand is posh. As in, I feel like an imposter

walking in with my scuffed handbag and laddered tights. But once I sit down at the glossy black Steinway in the atrium and start playing, I forget all that. For three hours I'm background music for honeymooners, businessmen, and wealthy ladies nibbling cucumber sandwiches. Sometimes I slip in *Ave Maria* when I'm feeling particularly Catholic, but mostly it's Chopin or *Moon River*.

Except today, while I was halfway through Debussy, the General Manager, Mr Carrow, came sweeping past, gave me a look, and mouthed, *Not that one.*

What's wrong with Debussy?! It's not like I was pounding out "Great Balls of Fire"!

So, I stopped abruptly, which was terribly awkward because everyone looked up at once, and I panicked and launched into *Ode to Joy*. Except I got the tempo all wrong, and it ended up sounding like a funeral march.

So that went well.

4th September

Confession time (not sacramental - just me being honest with myself): I covet.

I covet fireplaces. Warm, crackling, toasty fireplaces in snug living rooms with bookcases and tartan rugs. I keep seeing them on Pinterest, all styled with pumpkin garlands and saint statues tastefully arranged on the mantel. Meanwhile, my flat has one radiator that clanks like it's rehearsing for a percussion section.

My piano students do not help with this problem. Today,

little Oliver came for his lesson, and his mum casually mentioned that their "new cottage" has "the cutest inglenook fireplace." I nearly expired from envy. It's not very holy of me, but I consoled myself by remembering that St Thérèse probably didn't have central heating either.

8th September

Marian Feast Day! Mary's birthday, which I celebrated by wearing a blue dress (and by not spilling coffee down it until lunchtime, which I feel is practically a miracle).

Work was chaotic. A wedding party has checked into the Wisteria Grand, and apparently they expect *live* music at every possible moment. Walking down the staircase? Live music. Cutting the cake? Live music. Someone sneezes? Better play *Pachelbel's Canon*.

The groom's aunt cornered me and asked if I could play *All You Need Is Love* like in *Love Actually*, with a brass band magically appearing. I said, "Of course!"- because I'm trying to practise Christian kindness - but what I meant was, *Madam, I'm one woman and a piano, not Paul McCartney plus twenty trumpeters.*

Still, I played it. And it was fine until I accidentally segued into *God Rest Ye Merry, Gentlemen* (wrong key, don't ask). Everyone looked startled, but I smiled serenely, like, *Yes, of course we'll now have a Christmas interlude in September, isn't that exactly what you ordered?*

9th September

The thing is, I *am* trying to be good.

I'm trying to see Christ in every guest, even the ones who complain that their scones are "too floury" (honestly, what does that even mean?). I'm trying to make my music prayerful, even when people treat me like an expensive Spotify playlist.

And yet.

This morning, I arrived late, tripped over a ficus plant in the lobby and scattered my sheet music everywhere. And, right as I was frantically scrambling to pick it all up, a man I'd never seen before stooped down and helped me.

Tall. Dark-haired. Grey suit. Smelled faintly of cedarwood and soap.

"Are you all right?" he asked.

And what did I do? I said, "Yes, thank you, I'm training for the Olympics."

Olympics.

Why.

He raised an eyebrow, handed me my crumpled Chopin, and walked away before I could explain. I offered that little humiliation up, but I still spent the next hour replaying it in my head, like a badly edited film reel.

12th September

Guess who turned up again today?

Yes. Mr Cedarwood-and-Soap.

I was in the atrium, playing *Clair de Lune* (which, apparently, is "allowable" according to Mr Carrow's mysterious musical rules), when I glanced up and there he was, leaning on the reception desk, talking to the concierge.

He caught my eye, smiled, and then - horror of horrors - I lost my place. Which is not something you can do in *Clair de Lune*. You can't just restart, like "Oops, never mind, let's go back to bar thirty." It's all atmosphere and rippling notes, and once you fumble, it's like watching someone fall off a tightrope in slow motion.

So, I did what any professional would do: I started playing *Twinkle, Twinkle, Little Star*. With *absolute confidence*.

And you know what? A little girl in a pink dress clapped. So that was fine.

But, when I glanced up again, Mr Cedarwood-and-Soap was definitely laughing. Not in a mean way. In an amused way. Which, for some reason, made me blush like I'd just been caught playing *Chopsticks* at the Royal Albert Hall.

15th September

My bank account and I had a serious talk today.

The bank account said, "Ha! Good luck buying groceries."

I said, "Don't be sarcastic."

It's true though - I'm behind on rent and lessons have been thin on the ground. Everyone seems to be away in Italy or Majorca. I stood outside a cottage estate agent's window this morning and gazed longingly at the sort of homes I dream about: fireplaces, beams, even window boxes with geraniums.

Then, I remembered my bank account and bought a reduced tin of soup instead. Holiness and humility in practice.

17th September

Sunday. Mass at St Mary's. I wore my green skirt and remembered not to sing the Gloria too enthusiastically (the last time, Mrs Turner gave me a look that suggested I was auditioning for *Britain's Got Talent*).

I'd just settled into my pew when - guess who walked in?

Mr Cedarwood-and-Soap.

At Mass.

I nearly fell over in shock. (Honestly, I do an awful lot of nearly falling over.)

He genuflected properly, slipped into a pew across the aisle and prayed with that calm, serious expression of someone who knows what they're doing. I was instantly flustered. Do I look holy enough? Am I holding my missal upside down? Is my hair sticking out like a wild thicket?

Afterwards, he was chatting with Father James near the door, and I may or may not have pretended to tie my shoelace for *far too long* in order to overhear. All I caught was "new to the area" and "business consultant."

So. He's real. He's local. He goes to Mass. And he has excellent aftershave.

20th September

Disaster.

Today, Mrs Peabody, a very prestigious regular guest at the Wisteria Grand, requested that I play "something suitably uplifting for her bridge club."

I thought she meant Bach.

She meant Abba.

So, there I was, trying to make *Dancing Queen* sound dignified on the Steinway, when - of course - Mr Cedarwood-and-Soap walked past again. He stopped, listened, and - oh yes - started clapping along.

So, now he's not only seen me Olympic-training-with-sheet-music, and butchering *Clair de Lune*, but also transforming into the world's most awkward one-woman Abba tribute act.

Dear Diary, pray for me.

22nd September

It happened.

I finally found out Mr Cedarwood-and-Soap's name.

Are you ready?

It's *John*.

Which is excellent because:
1.   Gospel writer/Jesus' best friend. ☑
2.   Easy to spell. ☑
3.   I can imagine shouting it across a windswept field and it would sound very dramatic. ☑

How do I know this? Because today I was *introduced*.

It all began with another ficus incident. (Why is there always a ficus? Do hotels import them specifically to trip me up?) I was trying to edge discreetly around it with my music bag when - surprise, surprise - I clipped the pot, lurched sideways, and practically threw myself into John.

"Ah," said the concierge, appearing magically at my elbow. "Miss Hartley, this is Mr John Davenport, one of our long-term corporate guests."

Corporate guest. Of course. He looks like the sort of man who has important meetings with leather-bound notebooks and decisive handshakes.

I smiled, still half-embedded in the ficus. "Lovely to meet you."

And then, because I panic in social interactions, I added, "I don't usually crash into plants like that."

Yes. Smooth.

He just grinned. "I'll take your word for it."

23rd September

Financial update: still broke.

This morning, while playing during breakfast service, I tried not to covet the croissants that guests left untouched on their plates. Do you think it's wrong to rescue pastries? I mean, waste is sinful, right?

On the bright side, little Oliver's mum has booked an *extra* piano lesson for him this week, which means I might actually be able to afford the nicer tea bags instead of the off-brand ones that taste like boiled socks. God provides - even in Yorkshire Tea.

24th September

Sunday again. Mass was beautiful: crisp sunlight through stained glass, the smell of incense, Father James giving a homily about gratitude. (Note to self: must stop mentally composing shopping lists during homilies. Very ungrateful behaviour.)

And afterwards - John was there again. He even helped stack chairs after coffee. Imagine! A man in a tailored suit putting away folding chairs. I didn't think they came in that edition.

He said hello this time. Properly. "You're the pianist at the hotel, aren't you?"

I squeaked (yes, squeaked) something like "Yesbutlalsogivelessons" and immediately wanted to die. But then he surprised me:

"My mum's been saying she wants to take up piano again. Maybe I should mention you."

WHAT.

So, now I've gone from humiliating myself with ficuses to potentially gaining a new student. Which just goes to show that God does indeed write straight with very crooked lines.

27th September

Today, I had what can only be described as *a major professional incident.*

I was in the atrium, doing my usual "calm background piano while people sip tea and pretend not to eavesdrop on each others' conversations" routine. All was going well. I was midway through *Moon River*.

Then suddenly, without warning, the fire alarm went off.

Now, a normal person would stop playing and evacuate. Sensible. Logical.

I, however, froze in sheer panic. And what did my fingers do? They kept playing. Faster. Louder. Until *Moon River* turned into something like a Liszt concerto on caffeine.

Everyone evacuated while I, like I was auditioning for the soundtrack of the apocalypse, hammered out show tunes in an empty atrium. Finally, a staff member came sprinting in and yelled, "Miss Hartley, you need to *leave the piano.*"

So I did. With great dignity, of course.

Later, it turned out it was just burnt toast in the kitchen.

And, when we all trooped back inside, guess who smirked at me like he'd thoroughly enjoyed the show? Yes. John Davenport.

29th September

Feast of Saints Michael, Gabriel and Raphael, Archangels! (I remembered to put a little prayer card by the piano before work. Very discreet. Felt instantly fortified.)

The hotel is swarming with guests again because of some forestry conference. (Yes, really. Apparently, people get together to talk about oak trees and sustainable woodland. Who knew?)

I was playing discreetly in the corner, when John sat down nearby with a coffee. He stayed the entire time. Didn't pretend to read the paper. Didn't take out his phone. Just… listened.

At the end, he said quietly, "That was beautiful. You play with so much heart."

Reader, I nearly fell off the piano stool.

1st October

New month. Fresh start. (Fresh bank balance? Ha! Don't be ridiculous.)

After Mass, I walked home through the woods and, honestly, the New Forest is showing off. Gold and russet leaves everywhere, ponies cropping grass by the roadside, the smell of woodsmoke drifting from cottages. It made me long for one of those fireplaces again. If I had a log basket and a tartan rug, I'd never complain about anything again. (Well… maybe about tights that ladder within five minutes. Even saints must have limits.)

3rd October

Disaster at the hotel.

Mr Carrow asked me to "play something atmospheric" in the atrium. I thought he meant Chopin. He meant *Enya*.

So, while I was floating away in a cloud of delicate nocturnes, he stormed over and hissed, "Where is the *Enya* vibe?"

Enya vibe? I don't have an internal fog machine or a choir of mystical voices on standby.

In the end, I tried humming along to make it sound more ethereal, which unfortunately made it sound like I was auditioning for *Phantom of the Opera*.

And yes. John was there. Laughing silently into his coffee.

4th October

Small miracle: John actually came over and talked to me properly, after I finished playing.

"Do you always hum when you perform?" he asked, deadpan.

I immediately blurted out, "Only when I'm praying!" which was not *entirely* true, but sounded so impressively pious that I may keep it as my official line.

Then he said something that made my knees wobble like blancmange: "Well, I thought it was charming."

Reader, is this… flirting? Do Catholic men flirt? No one ever told me the protocol.

6th October

Here's the twist.

I was happily teaching little Oliver his scales this morning when his mum breezed in and said, "Oh, you'll never guess who I ran into at the hotel last week - my cousin, John Davenport!"
I stared at her. "Your… cousin?"

Yes. Cousin. As in related. As in *John-who-smells-of-cedarwood-and-makes-my-heart-go-wibbly* is **Oliver's cousin**.

Which means:
1.   His family probably already knows I charge £12.50 an hour and occasionally accept payment in tins of biscuits.
2.   He could, at any moment, sit in on one of Oliver's lessons.
3.   I might actually die.

I smiled bravely and said, "Oh! Small world!" while internally screaming.

7th October

I did not die. But close.

This afternoon, I was giving Oliver his lesson when the doorbell rang - and who was standing there? Yes. John Davenport. Holding a box of biscuits.

"Thought I'd bring these for my cousin's teacher," he said casually, as though he weren't delivering my imminent nervous breakdown in a cardboard tin.

I went bright red, nearly dropped my metronome on my foot, and muttered, "I don't usually accept biscuits from corporate guests."

WHAT.

Why do I *say these things?*

He just smiled. "Good thing I'm also family, then."

Help.

8th October

Mass this morning and I'm not saying I deliberately picked a pew where John might see me, but... let's just say I had an excellent view of him lighting a candle afterwards.

He looked so thoughtful, so prayerful, that I had a ridiculous little moment of imagining us married, with three children in tow, singing *Be Thou My Vision* while I play the organ.

And then I tripped over the kneeler on my way out and nearly flattened Mrs Turner.

So. Back to earth.

12th October

Surprise gig: a Very Important Conference Dinner at the hotel. Mr Carrow informed me I would be playing "discreetly, but with flair." (What does that *mean*? Am I supposed to play Chopin while juggling maracas?)

Halfway through, John appeared and - would you believe it - actually requested a piece. Not Abba. Not Enya. He asked for *Be Thou My Vision*.

So, there I was, in a posh hotel dining room full of forestry experts and businessmen, playing a hymn. And it was beautiful. And John smiled at me the whole way through.

I think my heart might have combusted quietly on the spot.

14th October

Disaster. Financial disaster.

I sat down this morning with my bank statement and a cup of tea, and nearly choked on the teabag (I had to reuse one for economy).

The numbers do not add up. In fact, they're practically dancing around the page, jeering at me. Rent due. Piano tuning overdue. Radiator still making death-rattle noises.

I did a quick calculation: if I stop buying tea, biscuits, and tights, I might survive until Christmas. (Although one could argue that life without tea and biscuits isn't really survival.)

Prayed a rosary for financial miracles. St Joseph, patron saint of workers, please send either more students or a winning lottery ticket.

18th October

Today, *the misunderstanding.*

I was playing in the atrium when two ladies at the next table began whispering about "Mr Davenport's fiancée."

Fiancée.

I nearly missed the entire second page of Chopin.

Of course, I smiled serenely and carried on, but inside I was shrieking: *He has a fiancée? He's engaged? Why is God playing with me like this?*

Afterwards, I practically bolted home, flung myself on the sofa, and had a very dramatic conversation in front of my Lourdes candle.

"Fine, Lord. If he's engaged, I will accept it. Thy will be done. But honestly, a little warning would have been nice."

19th October

Update: apparently John does *not* have a fiancée.

How do I know? Because Oliver's mum came for tea this afternoon and casually said, "Isn't it nice John's helping his sister plan her wedding?"

Sister.

Not fiancée. Sister.

So, while I was busy offering up my broken heart for the souls in Purgatory, he was just being a normal, supportive brother.

Moral of the story: never eavesdrop. It leads to melodrama, tea stains, and rosaries rattled off like an auctioneer on rocket fuel.

22nd October

Harvest Festival at St Mary's!

I love it - baskets of apples and squash, jam jars with gingham lids, the smell of chrysanthemums. I played the piano for the children's choir, which went fairly smoothly until one little boy started bellowing "All Things Bright and Beautiful" at twice the speed of everyone else.

John was there. He helped carry crates of vegetables to the altar. He smiled at me afterwards and said, "You make even hymn practice look fun."

I am beginning to suspect he actually likes me.

24th October

Another humiliation at the hotel.

I was asked to play something "autumnal" for a special dinner. I thought Vivaldi's *Autumn* would be perfect. Unfortunately, halfway through, I got lost in the repeats and ended up in *Winter* without warning.

So, one moment it was all harvest joy and merriment, the next it was bleak midwinter and death by snowstorm.

A couple of guests actually shivered.

And yes. John was there. Applauding with great enthusiasm, as though I'd just done it deliberately for effect.

25th October

Financial crisis update: I may actually have to sell my spare music stand.

But then - miracle! - John's mother rang me. (Yes, his mother.) Apparently, John mentioned me, and she wants piano lessons.

So, not only might I get a new student, but I might also get to meet his entire family. Which is terrifying and thrilling in equal measure.

I have exactly four days to learn how to appear like a competent, financially stable professional who never once reheated soup three nights running.

26th October

John's mum arrived for her first lesson today. She is absolutely lovely: warm, chatty and asked me at least four times if I was, "managing all right on your music income, dear."

I smiled bravely and said, "Yes, perfectly fine," while hoping she wouldn't notice the slightly peeling wallpaper behind the piano.

Then, as she left, she patted my hand and said, "John's right about you. You've got such a gift."

WHAT DID HE SAY ABOUT ME?!

31st October

All Hallows' Eve. (I've decided to prepare for All Saints' with great holiness and definitely not eat the reduced-price toffee apples I found at Tesco until tomorrow. Absolutely not.)

This afternoon, John stopped by while I was teaching. He waited in the kitchen, drinking tea, until I finished. And when Oliver left, John said, "So. Any chance you'd like to walk in the forest with me tomorrow? Just… a proper autumn walk."

Dear Diary, I think I may have just fallen headfirst into something rather wonderful.

1st November - All Saints 'Day

Glorious feast day and holy day of obligation! I went to morning Mass, and the church looked so beautiful with candlelight flickering on the cream-coloured walls. I wore my blue scarf and tried to look suitably saintly (ignoring the fact that I'd sprinted the last hundred yards because I was late again).

Afterwards, John caught up with me in the churchyard. "Still training for the Olympics?" he teased. (Yes, he remembers my original humiliation. Of course he does.)

We walked through the woods afterwards, and it was golden. Fallen leaves crunching underfoot, shafts of sunlight through beech trees, ponies wandering as if they'd been hired by a film set. And for a moment, I thought: *This feels like something out of a novel.*

Then, I promptly tripped on a tree root, stumbled into John, and somehow we both ended up laughing so hard we had to lean on the same tree to recover. Honestly. Smooth as butter, me.

3rd November

Financial situation: dire.

I opened my cupboard this morning and discovered three tins of chickpeas, half a jar of marmalade, and some stale crackers. This is not a meal plan: this is an ordeal.

So, I did what any good Catholic girl would do: lit a candle, prayed to St Joseph, and made chickpea soup. Again.

Meanwhile, the Wisteria Grand has decided that the piano in the atrium is "under review." Mr Carrow muttered something about "budget realignment", which I think means they might replace me with a CD player.

A CD player! In 2025! I nearly fainted.

5th November

Sunday Mass. Afterwards, the parish hall hosted its annual "Soup and Social". Everyone brought soup. There were fifteen varieties lined up on the counter, and yes, mine was chickpea.

The twist? John took a spoonful of mine, paused, and said, "This is really good. What do you put in it?"

Reader, I nearly burst into tears on the spot. Because the honest answer is "desperation and slightly out-of-date cumin". But instead, I smiled serenely and said, "It's a family recipe."

9th November

The Twist.

This morning, as I was teaching Oliver, John appeared early. He hovered in the kitchen, drinking tea, until the lesson ended. Then he said, "There's something I'd like to ask you."

Cue my heart doing somersaults.

He cleared his throat. "Would you be interested in... teaching me?"

Teaching him. Piano.

I blinked. "You want piano lessons?"

He grinned. "Why not? I've always wanted to learn. And I've been watching you play... you make it look like more than music. Like prayer."

Well. At that point, I just about melted into the carpet. But I rallied and said, "Of course. Although, fair warning, I'm a very strict teacher."

To which he replied, dead serious: "Good. I need someone to keep me in line."

I may combust.

13th November

First piano lesson with John.

Disaster.

I tried to be professional, truly I did. I sat down with my teaching book, explained finger positions, and said briskly, "Now, let's try middle C."

He looked at me, grinned, and deliberately pressed *every other key but middle C.*

"Wrong note?" he asked, eyes twinkling.

I snorted with laughter so loudly that Oliver's mum, who was waiting outside, poked her head in to see if I was choking.

So much for professionalism.

15th November

Another crisis.

I was summoned to Mr Carrow's office at the Wisteria Grand. He gave me the "budget realignment" talk again, then said, "We may have to cut live music. Unless…"

Unless what?

"Unless you're willing to provide... a bit more variety."

Which is how I now find myself committed to playing not only classical, but also jazz, film soundtracks, and - Heaven help me - Disney medleys.

Yes. Disney. In a five-star hotel atrium.

Pray for me.

20th November

Today, John came to his lesson, sat down at the piano, and said, "Play something first. Please. Just for me."

So, I played *Soul of my Saviour* softly, and, when I finished, the room was completely quiet.

Then he said, "You really are remarkable."

Reader, I think he might mean it.

22nd November

Mr Carrow has announced a "Special Gala Evening" at the hotel: champagne, fancy canapés, Very Important Guests. My role? To provide "varied, elegant, family-friendly entertainment."

Which is a managerial way of saying: *don't mess up, Hartley.*

Naturally, I am already panicking.

23rd November

Rehearsed for hours today. Classical pieces ✓, jazzy pieces ✓, Disney medleys ✓. (Yes, Disney. I've now learned that *A Whole New World* can, in fact, be made to sound like Chopin. You just have to commit.)

John stopped by for his "lesson," which turned into him teasing me relentlessly about playing *Frozen* for aristocrats. "If you get them all singing *Let it go*, I'll be impressed."

Ha. Ha.

25th November - Gala Night

Disaster.

Absolute, unmitigated disaster.

I began well - Chopin nocturnes, Debussy ripples, a bit of jazz. Everyone nodded approvingly. Then Mrs Peabody (why always Mrs Peabody?) tottered over and said, "Do be a darling and play something from *The Sound of Music*."

Fine. Lovely. I launched into *My Favourite Things*.

Only then, the head waiter tripped over a champagne bucket, the cork flew straight into the chandelier and, in the chaos, I completely lost my place and somehow segued into *Let it go*.

Yes. In front of lords, ladies, forestry magnates, and Mr Carrow himself, I played *Let it go*.

And then - THEN - the entire children's table started singing along. With hand gestures.

So, there I was, a lone pianist leading an impromptu Disney singalong in a five-star New Forest hotel.

I wanted the ground to swallow me whole.

Later, same night

But here's the miracle: it worked.

Instead of glaring, the guests *loved it*. They laughed, clapped and even Mr Carrow admitted it "brought warmth to the evening."

And John? John stood at the back of the room, arms folded, grinning at me like I was the cleverest girl in the world.

Afterwards he found me, still red-faced, and said, "See? I told you *Let it go* would win them over."

I groaned. "I'll never live this down."

He smiled. "I hope not."

26th November

Sunday. Christ the King. The choir was in full voice, the incense was beautiful and Father James preached about joy.

Afterwards, John walked me home through the woods. The leaves are nearly all gone now, branches stark against the sky, the air smelling of frost.

He carried my music bag for me and halfway down the path he said quietly, "You know… you've made this place feel more like home for me."

And I, in a burst of accidental honesty, said, "You've made it feel more like a dream for me."

Then blushed furiously.

He didn't laugh. He just smiled and we walked on in silence and the silence was… perfect.

28th November

Financial crisis update: still hanging by a thread. Chickpeas are featuring too heavily in my life.

But you know what? I'm strangely… peaceful.

Maybe it's the prayers. Maybe it's autumn in the forest. Maybe it's John.

Probably all three.

30th November

Feast of St Andrew. I said Morning Prayer with extra fervour, mostly because I needed strength after the chickpea-soup marathon of recent weeks.

The Wisteria Grand was quiet today, the last of the leaves blowing across the gravel drive like fiery embers. I played softly in the atrium - hymns woven into Chopin, because no one really notices and it felt right.

John came in, sat down nearby and just listened. Afterwards, he said, "I could listen to you play all day." His eyes didn't stay on the piano - they stayed on me, calm and kind, with that mix of warmth and mischief that makes you feel like he actually notices *everything* about you. My heart gave a very inconvenient lurch.

Okay, today is St Andrew's Day - courage, remember? So, I swallowed hard, straightened my shoulders and kept playing, even though my fingers were threatening to stage a rebellion.

Leaning just slightly closer, he said, "I know I can't *actually* listen all day - business meetings await - but… would you like to have dinner with me this Friday - tomorrow - evening? Proper dinner. No piano required."

Reader, I nearly hit a high note in panic and delight at the same time.

I blinked at him, trying to look calm and sophisticated, which, given my current state of internal chaos, was probably laughable. "Dinner?" I squeaked. Very dignified. Very composed.

He gave a small, warm smile - the kind that somehow made it feel like he could see all the ridiculous thoughts running through my head and still like me anyway. "Friday," he said. "After you finish - eight-thirty sound good?"

I nodded, because apparently *not fainting* was the only heroic thing I could manage. "I… I'd like that," I said, trying not to squeak again.

He gave a small, teasing shrug - that impossible mix of calm and mischief that somehow made me feel noticed, flustered, and ridiculously delighted all at once. But, hang on a minute, was he actually *blushing*??

He soon left for his important business meetings and I stayed at the piano for a few more minutes, idly drumming the keys while my mind ran wild imagining what to wear. Reader, my wardrobe is... generous only in imagination. My best skirt has a tiny hole near the hem, my blouses are either too big or slightly pink from last week's beetroot disaster and my shoes squeak like they're gossiping about me.

Later, same day

I've finally settled on a plan of sheer genius: I'll wear my blue cardigan over the skirt, tuck in my blouse as best I can and strategically place a scarf - borrowed from my aunt years ago - to draw attention *away from the hole*. Voilà. Instant elegance. And if anyone asks, the squeaky shoes? "Deliberate vintage chic," I'll say.

As I twirled in front of the mirror, piano sheet music balanced precariously on the edge of the dresser, I imagined John's face, faintly blushing and slightly amused. Reader, I think my pulse just composed its own little jazz improvisation of nerves and glee.

Also, while thinking about what to wear, I suddenly had the most brilliant idea: **piano lessons via video call**! Charge a proper rate, no travel and I could actually save for a real fireplace. Genius, right?

Must look into feasibility of this. Immediately.

Dear St Joseph, please work your wonders.

2nd December

Dear Diary,

I think I'm still floating.

Dinner with John wasn't candlelit violins and roses - it was better. It was the most delicious fish and chips I've ever had - at a quiet country pub, with a shared crumble for dessert, and soft jazz playing in the background while we talked about everything and nothing.

He didn't bring roses. He brought a second-hand copy of *The Wind in the Willows*, with a note inside: *"For your future fireplace. And your bookshelf beside it."*

I didn't cry. But I thought about it.

We talked about faith and music, and my eternal struggle with tights. He told me he's considering staying in the area long-term and when I joked that he was just here for the chickpea soup, he said, "Well, that. And you."

Reader, I dropped my spoon.

When he walked me home through the frosty dark, the stars were out and I could see my breath puffing in front of me. At my front door, he hesitated - like in every cheesy movie ever - and then said, "I know this is still new, and I don't want to rush anything. But… I really like you."

And I - well, I said, "I really like you too." And then I

accidentally kicked the doormat. But he just laughed and kissed me lightly on the cheek.

And there it was. Soft. Simple. Honest. Like the first chord of a hymn you already know by heart.

I went inside, took off my squeaky shoes, and just stood in the middle of the room for a moment, heart pounding like a timpani.

No, I don't have a fireplace yet.

Yes, my tights still ladder.

And I'm probably one soggy cracker away from financial collapse.

But I have music. And faith. And - maybe - a future that smells faintly of cedarwood and starts with middle C.

Reader, I think this might just be the prelude.

The Cocoa Hare's Advent Escapade

If you have never been to Much Marvingstowe in December, imagine a village that looks as if it has been knitted by a particularly sentimental grandmother, perhaps even by Old Mrs Biddle herself. Thatched roofs and stone walls in a shade that falls somewhere between warm toast and ginger biscuit and the ancient Eleanor Cross standing only a mince-pie's throw away, like a grand old dowager who knows the best gossip, but won't tell. At twilight, a gentle hush settles over the quietly magical lanes. The cottages - plum puddings in architectural form - trimmed with modest fairy lights, twinkle softly as if blushing under the gaze of passing carol singers.

Into this frosted idyll had recently arrived Carlo and Gemma Becket - newlyweds and proprietors of *The Cocoa Hare*, a chocolate shop whose displays could make even the most disciplined dentist reconsider their calling. As it turned out, the Beckets were not entirely ready for the sort of Yuletide mêlée that descends upon an English village in the weeks before Christmas. They had been assured by well-meaning locals that Christmas retail in Much Marvingstowe was "lively, but manageable." Which is rather like saying that Everest is "a touch steep" or that the North Sea in January is "brisk".

On the Tuesday in question, Carlo was attempting to stack a display of marzipan reindeer, positioning himself at a very awkward angle that foretold future physiotherapy appointments, when in burst Colonel Tibbets, late of the Royal Engineers, booming for a "pound of that *Bethlehem Brittle* - the stuff that nearly cracked my dentures last year. Splendid!"

Carlo gave a startled twitch and several reindeer resigned from their posts, cartwheeling into the tinsel with soft thuds.

"Here you go, Colonel," he said, smiling jauntily and handing over a bag of *Bethlehem Brittle*. "Just watch your teeth on this batch."

"Quite so!" barked the Colonel. "If the Queen'd had brittle like this during the war, we'd have taken Berlin by Easter. Of course, I'm not at liberty to discuss the brittle-related operations of '43. Classified, you understand."

Colonel Tibbetts had been followed into the chocolate shop at close quarters by Mrs Cressida Plum, chairwoman of the Much Marvingstowe Amateur Dramatic Society, who wished to know why the Beckets' chocolate Nativity scene had three kings, but no shepherds. "It's not doctrinally balanced," she sniffed.

"We had shepherds," said Gemma brightly, "but someone ate them. Then, interestingly, we had some *German* shepherds, but someone ate them too."

"Really, my dear," said Mrs Plum, scandalised. "That is not theologically sound."

Before Gemma could respond, the shop door banged open again and young Michael Donnelly slouched in, looking like a cat that had just lost an argument with a rain barrel.

"No Christmas at ours," he announced glumly. "Dad says the money's gone on the boiler."

Gemma, who could not see a child in distress without

producing sugar in some form, darted behind the counter and returned with a small paper bag of Eleanor Cross bars and some cinnamon truffles.

"Tell your dad," she said, "this is from us. And that *Emmanuel* means *God with us* - even when the boiler's being a nuisance."

Michael took the bag slowly. "Thanks, Miss. Mum says chocolate doesn't solve everything, but…" He peered in. "She hasn't tried your truffles."

"I've got a feeling she ain't gonna be trying any of those either," whispered Carlo to Gemma as Michael ambled away, tucking in with the enthusiasm of a cocker spaniel at an unattended picnic basket.

Carlo had then become entangled in a conversation with Old Mr Sprockett, the village's unofficial historian, who was loudly insisting that the Roman aqueduct supposedly buried beneath the allotments was "responsible for Mrs Penrose's recurring dreams of fish." Carlo initially thought he was complaining about the plumbing, and promised to check the pipes.

The Cocoa Hare descended into a scene of genteel mayhem - Colonel Tibbets arguing with Mrs Plum about whether the Angel Gabriel had worn a helmet, Gemma fielding questions about whether chocolate coins could be made dairy-free for Mrs O'Reilly's cousin in Kettering, and Carlo chasing an escaped marzipan sheep that had been swiped from the Nativity by little Tommy Biddle.

"I'm borrowing it!" Tommy yelled as he ran, "It's for Baby Jesus!"

"Borrowing without asking is theft, Thomas!" said Old Mrs Biddle, firmly, not looking up from her knitting.

Carlo blinked. He was fairly sure Mrs Biddle hadn't been there two minutes ago and yet here she was: seated squarely in the middle of the shop, knitting with the serene intensity of someone who had *always* been knitting and would still be knitting long after the End Times. *Had she brought her own chair?*

Deeply reluctant to ask any questions that might unravel reality even further, Carlo - against his own wishes - let out an entirely involuntary, high-pitched, nervous laugh. Then, trying to pretend he hadn't, he crept round to the marzipan reindeer display, trusting, as ever, that his dear wife Gemma would appear and sort everything out. *Where was she?* he wondered, desperately. *She was here a minute ago.*

At that moment, a scuffle was beginning to brew, just outside, on the village green. Two members of the *Much Marvingstowe Morris Men* - rival factions, it was whispered, after last year's "interpretive stick flourish" controversy - had arrived to rehearse for the Christmas Fayre. The problem was, both believed themselves to be the lead jester. What began as light stick-tapping quickly escalated into a full-on standoff that could only be described as *Morris with malice*. The two men faced each other, eyes narrowed, shin bells jingling and handkerchiefs fluttering like battle flags in the wind. To say nothing of the pheasant feathers. A dog barked three times - the ancient signal that Morris law had been broken.

When Gemma reappeared behind the shop counter, Carlo gazed at her with relief.

"I'm so sorry," Gemma began, with an apologetic smile, "but I'd already got the giggles and then when you did that shriek-laugh I had to go out for a sec, I was laughing so much."

Her voice still wobbled with barely repressed mirth over the day's chaotic antics so far. Now seeing Mrs Biddle, still sitting there knitting in the middle of the chocolate shop, like a character from a lost Chekhov play, Gemma ran out the back again, stifling fresh paroxysms of laughter. "Sorry! Sorry!" she called out as steadily as she could.

Six minutes later, just when it seemed they might get through the rest of the day without further drama, calamity arrived by the van-load - quite literally.

Mrs Penrose burst in, announcing that the Beckets' final Christmas delivery had been spotted on its side near Delapré Abbey, scattering boxes of *Bethlehem Brittle* along the verge "like manna from Heaven". One struck a bystander, who reportedly shouted 'Finally!' and vanished into the hedge.

"I was on the number 11 bus," she panted, "and I saw it. Boxes! Everywhere! The driver was on the phone, 'looking as distressed as a ferret wearing tap shoes during a silent retreat' - as the old family saying goes."

Carlo had heard this saying only once before, from a passing Jesuit. He dashed to the telephone, only to get connected to a bewildered garden ornament shop in Milton Keynes.

"Hello?" he asked, "Is this St Agnes Couriers?"

"You've reached Gnome Zone," said a voice. "We specialise in miniature windmills."

Gemma, left to hold the fort, found herself fending off Mrs Plum (now demanding marzipan ducks for the Nativity) and Colonel Tibbets, who had somehow acquired the village's 'live Nativity' donkey and was offering it a sample of *Eleanor Cross bars*.

"You see, animal bonding is all about shared rations," the Colonel explained, his voice booming.

The donkey, unimpressed, bolted through the shop door, upsetting the marzipan display and thundered off toward the village green with Carlo - phone call abruptly ended - in hot pursuit. This led to a case of mistaken identity when Mrs O'Reilly, seeing Carlo charging after a large four-legged shape, concluded he was chasing her St Bernard, Alfred, and joined the pursuit shouting, "Don't hurt him - he's teething!"

As the three of them cantered along, skirting the Morris dance of doom on the village green, an angry roar of "Artistic betrayal!!" pierced the air, followed by a violent clack of Morris sticks and the jingling of shin bells. Carlo, casting a glance over his shoulder, noticed the onlookers were gripped in a collective crisis of conscience, unsure whether they should applaud or step in before someone was struck senseless by a rogue tambourine.

Meanwhile, back in the *The Cocoa Hare*, Mr Sprockett accused Gemma of concealing his missing Christmas hamper "in a secret compartment behind the truffle display." This theory collapsed when the hamper was found under Colonel Tibbets 'greatcoat, where the Colonel insisted it had been "merely resting".

"You can't just *borrow* a hamper, Colonel," said Gemma.

"Ah, but I intended to *return* it," said the Colonel. "Eventually. After thorough inspection."

He was spared further questioning by the timely return of the runaway donkey, which wandered back unbothered and promptly attempted to devour the chocolate camel.

"Not the camel!" wailed Mrs Plum. "We *only* had the one!"

It was coaxed away only by a carefully laid trail of peppermint creams.

By the time the dust - and a fair amount of cocoa powder - had settled; by the time Mrs Biddle had gone home, leaving them a gorgeous freshly-knitted tea cosy; and by the time the shelves were restocked, the donkey had bolted yet again and Colonel Tibbets - astonishingly nimble - was thundering after it. Carlo, gazing on in bewilderment, began to wonder if chaos might simply be the local version of a housewarming in these parts.

The Cathedral Interlude

That evening, in need of a change of scenery, the Beckets drove into Northampton for evening Mass at the Catholic Cathedral. Technically a town - the largest in England without city status - Northampton felt a world away from Much Marvingstowe, but its closely packed terraced streets were aglow with a cheery patchwork of Christmas lights, with windows trimmed in warm reds and golds, blinking merrily into the dusk.

"There's a certain irony in leaving the countryside for the town just to find a bit of peace," Gemma whispered with a smile, as they crossed the dimly lit car park toward the cathedral doors.

They had brought a box of *Starry Chocolate Bites* as a small pre-Christmas gift in case they saw Ben and Nia, a couple they'd met a few Sundays ago in the cathedral's draughty side chapel while trying to locate the right hymn numbers. Their toddler, Elsie, had taken an instant liking to Gemma's handbag and refused to return it without a chocolate bribe - thus beginning what Ben cheerfully called "a promising inter-family alliance."

After Mass, the cathedral released its congregation into the cool night with quiet nods, murmured good nights and the barely-audible gasp of someone realising they'd left the oven on since lunch. Just as Carlo and Gemma were leaving, scanning the dwindling crowd for any sign of their friends, something utterly unexpected broke the stillness: the 'live Nativity' donkey - yes, that same hoofed delinquent from earlier - glided along past the cathedral like the swan from *Lohengrin*, with its air of mystical nobility, but significantly more droppings. A nun paused by the cathedral gates and crossed herself twice.

From a few streets behind, came the unmistakable bark of Colonel Tibbets, booming, "This is *exactly* how it started in Cairo!" as he gave chase (a statement which, like many of the Colonel's, was both context-free and likely slanderous).

Carlo and Gemma exchanged a glance and then burst out laughing with equal parts amusement and bemusement.

Moments later, a battered green Land Rover rounded the corner, crawling behind the donkey and the now-visible Colonel Tibbets, at a pace that could generously be described as philosophical. Behind the wheel sat Old Mr Sprockett, expression unreadable beneath his flat cap, a donkey trailer rattling emptily behind him. As he drew level with the cathedral car park entrance, he rolled down the window, gave a faint nod to the Beckets, saying simply, "Evenin' all," before drifting onward into the night, bringing up the rear of a thoroughly unauthorised carnival. In Much Marvingstowe, they called it Tuesday.

"Are you…*happy* with all of…this?" asked Carlo, hesitantly.

Gemma laughed. "Happy? I've never laughed so much in my life. The parish is lovely, the donkey's got a good turn of speed, and honestly? I think we might've landed somewhere special."

Carlo glanced at the donkey and its companions fading into the distance, then at Gemma, his beloved wife, smiling under the glow of the street lamps.

"Yeah," he said. "Me too."

Back in Much Marvingstowe, a lone Morris dancing handkerchief blew past their cosy chocolate shop window. Caught by a winter gust, its fluttering was accompanied by the faint shimmer of sleigh bells that carried through the night air - prompting young Michael Donnelly to ask his dad if that was Father Christmas on his way or if the maniacal Morris men were "still locked in their jingling death match".

Inside *The Cocoa Hare*, dark and closed for the night, the

only evidence of the day's escapades was a solitary Eleanor Cross bar left on the counter, as if it were waiting for a second act.

Christmas at Foxglove Hill

I should start by saying: I never meant to fall for James Ashbury. I was quite happy living my quiet little life, thank you very much. Well… quiet might be a bit generous. Chaotic-but-charming is probably more accurate.

I'm Ellie Mayfield, twenty-nine (although I do like to say "late twenties" to strangers), primary school teacher, and lifelong resident of Reedley - a blink-and-you'll-miss-it village tucked away among the flat, endless fields of rural Cambridgeshire. The kind where you can cycle for miles without a hill in sight, where the air always smells faintly of diesel from passing tractors, and the local postman, Harold, has stronger opinions about your dating life than your own mother.

This spring had arrived like something out of a Constable painting. The hedgerows were bursting with primroses, the fenland skies seemed impossibly wide and full of light, and you couldn't walk more than ten feet without tripping over a daffodil.

And right into all of this beauty - he arrived.

James Ashbury, London-born, sharply dressed, and annoyingly handsome in a rugged, I-chop-my-own-wood sort of way. He was the grandson of the late Lady Foxglove (real name: Alexandra Ashbury), who had left him the tumbledown manor at the top of the hill just beyond the village green. It had sat empty for years, ivy crawling over the stone walls as though it were trying to pull the place back into the earth.

"Probably here to sell it," muttered Mrs Pritchard, my

landlady-slash-village-gossip-column. "They never stay."

But James did stay. And he came to Mass that very first Sunday. Sat right at the back, looking completely lost in a sea of hymnals, flower arrangements, and Mrs Dennison's soprano solo during *Faith of Our Fathers* - which she treats more like an audition for *The X Factor* every time.

After Mass, I found myself being elbowed in his direction by my well-meaning friend Zita.

"Introduce yourself!" she whispered. "Be the welcoming committee!"

I didn't want to. I mean, what would we possibly have in common? He probably drank oat milk lattes and did yoga. But then he smiled - crooked, uncertain, a little tired - and I thought, *Fine. Just for a minute.*

"Hi," I said, holding out a hand. "Ellie Mayfield. I teach the Year Twos. Also lead the Easter bonnet parade, host the bake sale, and direct the Christmas Nativity, which once featured a live sheep and a fainting wise man."

He blinked. Then laughed. "I'm James. I inherited a crumbling mansion and a lot of broken teacups."

And that, somehow, was the beginning.

Over the next few weeks, James became something of a local curiosity. He fixed the gate at the church. Donated a whole stack of books to the village library (some were about theology, which made Father Sam beam for days). He even helped me carry eight dozen cupcakes to the school fête without once complaining about the glitter that got into his car.

We didn't exactly *date*. That would've been too obvious. But we… meandered. Through fields, down lanes, into moments that felt full of something I didn't have words for.

He told me about his mother, who'd raised him on her own in a flat in Islington and taught him to read the Psalms when he had nightmares.

I told him about my father, who always prayed before planting anything in the garden because he said God was the true gardener and what right did we have to mess it up?

And slowly, gently, something began to bloom.

It all came to a head one warm April afternoon, when the deacon's wife suggested James and I co-lead the children's Easter storytelling.

"I can't," I said quickly, panicked. "I'm not…"

"Not what?" James said later, as we walked through the apple orchard behind the church. "Not ready? Or not brave enough?"

I stopped walking. "I'm afraid to want something too much. What if I expect too much from God? What if I get it wrong?"

James was quiet for a moment. Then he said something I'll never forget.

"God doesn't ask us to be fearless, Ellie. He asks us to be faithful. Even when we're scared."

I looked at him then - really looked at him. And I saw someone who wasn't perfect, but who was willing to try. To grow. To build something real.

Foxglove Hill was blooming - literally and figuratively. The manor was being transformed (although James still refused to fix the squeaky stairs because they "have character"), the church was full every Sunday, and Mrs Dennison had thankfully toned it down to mezzo-soprano. I still led Easter bonnet parades, wrangled Year Twos, and sometimes, on quiet evenings under the cherry tree, James would read from the Psalms, softly, as though the words were meant just for us. And somehow, amidst all the chaos, love kept blooming.

And I thought, naively: *Well, that's it, then. Happy ending. Cue credits.*
Except life in Reedley doesn't work like that. You don't just get a spring romance and bow out gracefully. Oh no. Around here, stories roll on into fêtes, carol services and Father Sam's Labrador sabotaging everything in sight.

So, really, it was only a matter of time before love - and James - followed me straight into the most glitter-soaked, over-the-top season of all. Christmas.

Cue the tinsel and mayhem.

Reedley does Christmas like it's auditioning for *Britain's Most Festive Village*. Holly wreaths on every thatched cottage door. Fairy lights strung across the high street. Even the duck pond had its own floating Christmas tree (which promptly capsized after Father Sam's Labrador tried to chase a goose underneath it - cue Harold wading in with a fishing net and a look of long-suffering heroism).

My Year Twos were rehearsing the Nativity with alarming gusto. This year's Joseph had developed a strange habit of dabbing whenever he said his lines, the innkeeper kept announcing the "No room!" part as if auditioning for EastEnders and one of the shepherds produced a plastic lightsaber from his costume and tried to 'defend the flock'. I called it a success.

Meanwhile, James threw himself into the festivities like a man on a mission. He made wreaths out of actual holly from Foxglove Hill ("rustic chic", he claimed, though Mrs Pritchard said it looked like something the compost bin rejected, which I thought was a bit harsh). He strung fairy lights all around the outside of the presbytery, much to Father Sam's cautious amusement - though he reminded us that, technically, the lights could only shine after Midnight Mass, when it officially became Christmas, and not before. Naturally, James managed to blow a fuse and plunge the presbytery into darkness for three hours. Which is how I found myself sitting by candlelight with James, Father Sam, his Labrador, and his cat - basically handing Mrs Pritchard enough material to fuel the village gossip mill until Lent.

And then there was the carol-singing evening. Everyone came: the choir, the bell-ringers, even old Mr Beaton, who hasn't left his house since Gordon Brown was Prime Minister. James handed round mulled wine, mince pies, and (here's the kicker) gluten-free, vegan gingerbread men. Which I may or may not have burnt in the oven and then decorated to disguise the evidence. (In my defence, slightly charred gingerbread has depth of flavour. It's basically the single malt of biscuits. At least, that's what James claimed while discreetly spitting crumbs into a napkin.)

The point is: James looked completely at home, standing there with flour on his jumper, twinkle lights glinting behind him, chatting with everyone from Mrs Dennison to old Mr Beaton. And me? I stood in the corner, nibbling one of my own gingerbread prototypes, pretending not to be completely smitten.

On Christmas Eve, after midnight Mass - candlelight, pine, Father Sam practically weeping through *O Come All Ye Faithful* - James caught my hand.

"Come with me," he whispered.

Which sounded very romantic. Except I immediately panicked because I was still in my "church coat". You know the one: slightly puffy, suspiciously shiny, and makes me look like a walking black bin liner. Not exactly the look one hopes for in a sweeping romantic moment. But could I admit that? Of course not. I would rather face eternity in the world's puffiest coat than ruin whatever-this-was.

So, I followed him up the frosty lane to Foxglove Hill. And then - oh.

The cherry tree. He'd strung it with fairy lights, every branch glowing against the wide Fenland night sky. It looked like the heavens had spilled their stars just for us. My breath caught.

At that moment, in my attempt to look graceful and moved, I tried to perch daintily on the old bench… only to misjudge completely and nearly slide off sideways. Very dignified. (Although, in fairness, who puts a bench directly under twinkling lights without warning people to mind their balance?)

James didn't laugh. Well, not much. Instead, he dropped to one knee in the frost.

"Ellie Mayfield," he said, eyes steady on mine. "You bring light and joy wherever you go. I don't want this place to be just a house - I want us to make it a home. Together. Will you marry me?"

Now, I'd love to say I replied with elegant grace. But, in reality, my brain was too busy shrieking, *He said together. Together! Home! Marriage!* Also, I suddenly remembered I hadn't watered the poinsettia Zita gave me, and what sort of fiancée lets a plant die on Christmas Eve? Not a good omen at all. Best to say yes quickly, before anyone found out about the plant.

"Yes!" I blurted, far too loudly. "Yes, absolutely, definitely, completely yes!"

Then, I lunged into a hug so suddenly, I knocked my coat hood over his face and almost fell sideways off the bench. He caught me, laughing, as a half-decorated gingerbread man slid from my pocket and landed at his feet. The church bells rang out midnight behind us. Then, like someone had pressed "play" on a village-wide soundtrack, came a roar of cheering that could only mean one thing: Father Sam had finally flicked on the presbytery Christmas lights.

Because sometimes love is perfect. And sometimes it's slightly awkward, slightly chaotic, and wrapped in a puffa coat, with the whole village cheering in the background. But either way - it's Christmas. And it's ours.

Epilogue: Six Months Later

If you'd told me a year ago I'd be engaged to James Ashbury and planning a wedding at Foxglove Hill, I would have laughed politely and then hidden behind a tray of fairy cakes. But here we are. Engaged. In love. Wedding in three weeks.

And completely, utterly, catastrophically buried under tulle.

Honestly, the amount of *stuff* required for a wedding is insane. I have lists of lists. There's the dress list, the flowers list, the "what if it rains and everyone needs umbrellas in three different coordinating shades" list. And don't even get me started on the seating plan. (Why does Aunty Doreen hate Cousin Martin, and since when did Harold the postman suddenly require vegetarian carapés?)

But my pièce de résistance - my crowning achievement - is the bridesmaid capes. Yes, capes. Not shawls, not wraps. Actual satin-lined capes with hoods. Because when I first suggested it, everyone laughed. But then I said: *It'll look like Narnia meets Jane Austen meets Vogue.* And really, who wouldn't want that?

Of course, Zita did mutter something about it being "a bit Hogwarts", but I pointed out, very reasonably, that Hogwarts weddings would be extremely stylish if they ever happened. In fact, J.K. Rowling probably just hasn't got round to writing one. Zita's next words seemed to get lost somewhere between her brain and her mouth, which I counted as a win. Seizing the moment, I gave an exaggerated flourish with my imaginary cape, because if anyone was going to embrace Narnia-meets-Jane-Austen style, it was definitely me.

The only tiny hiccup so far was the cake tasting. Picture this: me, James, and three tiers of sample cake. I may have, in my enthusiasm, accidentally eaten most of the top tier before James had a chance to try it. Which I absolutely did *not* admit to. I told him Father Sam's cat had jumped on the table and - tragically - knocked it to the floor. Yes, fine, it was a lie. But technically not a full lie, because the cat *was* in the room. And also, who leaves me unattended with lemon drizzle cake? That's basically entrapment.

James, to his credit, just shook his head and kissed my icing-smeared cheek. He seems to think my wedding mania is endearing. (Either that, or he's too polite to say otherwise.)

Sometimes, in quieter moments, I sit with him under the cherry tree - now neatly pruned, twinkly lights packed away for next Christmas - and wonder how on earth I ended up here. In love, planning a life, preparing to say vows I once thought were for other people, braver people.

And then I remember: God doesn't ask us to be fearless. He asks us to be faithful. Even when you're terrified your bridesmaids are going to look like extras in a medieval fantasy film.

So, yes, maybe our wedding will feature capes, suspiciously eaten cake samples, and a seating plan drawn up like a UN peace treaty. But it will also feature James. And me. And a Catholic wedding in the village church, vows spoken under Fenland skies wide enough to hold all our messy, hopeful, imperfect love.

And really, what more could I possibly want?

The Loaf and the Lily

There are places on this Earth where time seems to saunter rather than sprint, and nowhere is that truer than in Somerset, where the hills roll like the folds of a woollen cloak and the wind carries the scent of hearth-smoke and wild rosemary. In the village of Thistledown - a name that sounds like it was plucked from a fairy tale and given to a post office by accident - life moves with a rhythm as old as the hedgerows, and just as beautiful. Thistledown is not on most maps, for the world has no time for such places anymore. But there it rests all the same, cradled between the ancient oaks of Somerset and the murmuring curves of the River Frome.

It was Advent, and winter had already begun laying her quiet claim to the land. The hedgerows were crisp with hoarfrost, the sheep huddled in little woolly congregations, and the skies turned from blue to smoky silver with a kind of sacred hush. The wind brought whispers of Christmas through the fields and the frost clung to the bare branches like silver thread.

Right at the heart of the village sat *The Loaf and the Lily,* a little bakery that looked as though it had grown there naturally - moss-kissed roof, warm brick walls, and windows always fogged with the scent of butter, cinnamon and good cheer. The bakery was not only famed for its cinnamon loaves and honeyed brioche, but for something rarer still: warmth, welcome, and the kind of peace that cannot be bought. Its windows glowed with golden light and people came from all over the countryside, not just for the bread, but for the sense of community, the laughter, and the quiet grace that seemed to hover in the air like a blessing.

The bakery was run by Miriam Fitzherbert, a widow who had lived through many seasons, many heartaches, and many joys. At seventy-two, her hair was as silver as the frost that kissed the hills at dawn, and her hands, lined by time, moved with the steady rhythm of a woman who had mastered the art of patience. Her smile was wide and her laugh deep, the kind that made you feel at home, no matter who you were.

Her bakery was her sanctuary, and the village - her family.

Miriam, keeper of the bakery, was already up before the light came. She moved with the deliberate ease of one who had made peace with the passing of time - and also knew precisely when the first batch of fig and walnut loaf should rise.

She stood in her kitchen with sleeves rolled to her elbows and her silver hair twisted up like an Elizabethan duchess - though one who wielded a rolling pin instead of a sceptre.

"The Lord sends His angels," she often said, "but He also sends warm bread."

Above her oven hung a hand-painted plaque:

"Man shall not live by bread alone, but by every word that proceedeth out of the mouth of God." - Matthew 4:4

Beneath it sat six trays of rising dough, each humming gently with promise.

Outside the bakery, the land sloped gently down to the river, where willows slept under their own frozen reflections. The fields, blanketed with frost, stretched out towards the distant hills, and the smoke from chimneys drifted lazily into the pale morning sky.

It was the second week of Advent; every window in the village was framed by holly and ivy, every doorstep lit by the warm glow of candlelight. The air had turned properly cold, and each morning brought a fresh dusting of snow. The church bells rang low across the valley, calling no one in particular and everyone at once.

Inside *The Loaf and the Lily*, Miriam was already at work, preparing for the weeks ahead. The ovens were on, and the air was filled with the fragrance of ginger, cinnamon, and nutmeg. There were mince pies to be baked, stollen to be iced, and fruitcakes that would soon be shared around dinner tables across the village.

Though Miriam worked alone in the early mornings, the bakery was never truly empty. There was always a stream of villagers who stopped by for a loaf of bread, a scone or just a bit of company.

That morning, as Miriam was shaping a batch of pains au chocolat, the door swung open, and in walked Eddie Young, the village postman. He was a jovial man, always with a smile on his face, though today he looked unusually frazzled.

"Morning, Miriam!" he called, rubbing his hands together against the cold. "Could I trouble you for a moment?"

Miriam didn't stop kneading. "You always trouble me, Eddie," she replied, her voice light. "What's going on now? Lost a parcel again?"

"Well, no," Eddie said, drawing closer to the counter. "This is more of a… church matter, actually."

"Church?" Miriam raised an eyebrow, but didn't look up. "Is Father Colin getting lost again? Last time he was at the village hall for an hour before someone pointed him in the right direction."

Eddie chuckled. "No, no. It's not Father Colin this time - it's the children. They've been practising for the Nativity, you know, but they're so excited about it, they're practically jumping out of their skins. The problem is, we're short of costumes, and I can't find the shepherds' robes anywhere. I've searched the church, the hall, the old shed… you name it."

Miriam stopped her work for a moment and looked up at Eddie. "Ah, that's what you're after, is it? Shepherds' robes?"

Eddie nodded, clearly at his wit's end. "Well, yes. I thought - seeing as you're so good with the sewing and all, maybe you could help?"

Miriam leaned back against the counter, crossing her arms. "I suppose I could. But only if you promise not to ask me to start a new choir next week."

Eddie grinned. "It's a deal. I'll bring the fabric."

"Good. Now go on, get out of here and let me get back to the important work," Miriam said, shooing him away with a flour-dusted hand.

Eddie winked, a familiar, warm presence in the doorframe. "I'll be back this afternoon. Thanks, Miriam. You're a lifesaver, as always."

As Eddie disappeared into the morning mist, Miriam smiled to herself and returned to her work. She had no doubt the costumes would be ready in time, as she had always managed to provide - whether it was food, a listening ear or, now, shepherds' robe for the village children.

The days leading up to Christmas in Thistledown were filled with the quiet busyness of preparation. Miriam baked into the evenings, her home and shop filled with the scents of Christmas. Each loaf of bread, each mince pie, each Christmas cake, was made with more than just ingredients - it was made with love, with a prayer that the coming of Christ would fill the hearts of all who came through her door.

And there were many who came.

There was Albert Jones, the widower who came for a loaf of bread each morning, though Miriam knew that what he was truly coming for was companionship. There was Mrs Morris, the elderly woman who sat by the fire, her hands shaking as she stirred her tea, telling stories of the old days when the bakery had been a much smaller place, before the war. And there were the children, laughing as they pressed their faces to the warm windows, hoping for a glimpse of the gingerbread men that Miriam had decorated that morning.

But of all the people who came through the doors of *The Loaf and the Lily*, none were more precious to Miriam than her great-niece Lucy, who had come back to Somerset from the bustling streets of Bristol. Lucy had always been the one to bring energy into a room, a spark of youth in an otherwise quiet place. She had a way of seeing the world with wonder, which, in turn, made the world seem a little more wondrous.

On the afternoon of Christmas Eve, as snow began to fall gently over the village, Lucy sat beside Miriam at the bakery's window, watching the village prepare for Midnight Mass.

"I've missed this," Lucy said softly, her breath fogging up the glass. "The quiet. The stillness."

Miriam smiled, her hands still busy with shaping a tray of mince pies. "The world always seems louder when we're far from home. But the quiet has its own kind of beauty, doesn't it?"

"Yes," Lucy agreed, her eyes drifting out towards the church. "It's like the whole village is preparing for something big, but it's all in silence. You know?"

Miriam nodded, brushing flour from her hands. "That's how Advent is meant to be, Lucy. It's a time of waiting. Not rushing. Not clamouring. Just waiting with an open heart."

Lucy paused, as if considering this. "I think that's what I needed. A little space. To listen."

The evening passed in a peaceful flurry. The bakery was a warm refuge for those who had finished their shopping, for families preparing for Mass. But as the clock struck midnight, Miriam locked the door, and she and Lucy walked to the church together, where the candles were lit and the scent of incense filled the air.

The church was bathed in the golden light of candles and the congregation stood close together, their voices rising in prayer. The sound of the bells, the voices of the faithful, the solemnity of the Mass - all of it swirled together in a holy unity that made the world outside seem far away.

Lucy stood beside Miriam, holding a candle, her heart quiet and full.

As they sang *Silent Night* together, the words of Isaiah 9:6 echoed in her mind:

'For unto us a child is born, unto us a son is given; and the government will be upon his shoulder: And his name shall be called Wonderful, Counsellor, Mighty God, Everlasting Father, Prince of Peace."

She looked at Miriam, whose hands were folded in prayer, and felt a deep sense of peace settle in her chest.

Later, back at the bakery, with the warmth of the fire crackling in the hearth, they sat together in comfortable silence. Lucy looked at the bread that had been carefully placed on the counter - loaves golden and fragrant, as they always were, loved by the village for their tenderness and sweetness.

But tonight, as the Christmas lights twinkled through the window and the stars sparkled softly above, it was a different kind of bread that occupied Lucy's thoughts. The Bread of Angels, *Panis Angelicus*, the Eucharist, the Bread that nourishes the soul in ways nothing on earth could. The simple joy of receiving Jesus in the Holy Sacrament, with a heart open and ready, was the true feast of the season.

In that quiet moment, with the glow of the Christmas lights casting a gentle, golden hue across the room, Lucy whispered a prayer of gratitude. The cottage outside was twinkling with delicate fairy lights, its windows filled with festive wreaths of holly and ivy and the scent of fresh pine wafted from the nearby trees. The soft glow of the candles on the windowsills mirrored the light in her heart, reflecting the gift of Christ, the true light of Christmas.

"Merry Christmas, Aunty Miriam," Lucy said softly, turning to her great-aunt, whose face was lit with the same peace that had filled their church.

"Merry Christmas, child," Miriam replied, her voice full of warmth and love. "May the peace of Christ fill you and all of us."

And in that moment, surrounded by the gentle glow of Christmas, with the flicker of the fire and the soft lilt of distant carols, Lucy understood - true joy comes not just from what we make, but from what has been given to us. The Bread of Angels, the love of Christ, and the warmth of family and friends - these were the gifts that would last long after the decorations were taken down.

The Christmas lights twinkled through the window, casting playful shadows across the snow-covered earth, and all around them, time itself seemed to slow, hushed in silent wonder.

The Narrow Way to Lakelore

It was in the curious interval between Christmas and New Year - a time when the world seems to be suspended between one miracle and the next - that Mr Ambrose Penfold found himself standing on the platform of the Lakelore Narrow Gauge Railway. The station was not large, nor did it pretend to be; it was more a cluster of timbered buildings, like old wooden teeth in a smiling jaw, and a single platform that seemed to lean toward the hills with a kindly, conspiratorial tilt. The snow had decided to arrive in little, discreet flurries, as though it were not daring to disturb the solemnity of this modest station.

Mr Penfold was a man of habitual devotions and habitual amusements. His piety was of a quiet, unassuming kind, the kind that preferred to slip into a pew unnoticed and leave with his conscience far lighter than when he arrived. Yet, he had a singular weakness for trains, particularly those with a nostalgic antiquity about them - trains that seemed to require prayer as much as coal. It was, he liked to say, impossible to have a bad thought aboard a steam engine. One could only pray, or whistle like a cheerful fool.

"Christmas train!" cried a portly ticket clerk, whose spectacles were fogged by the winter air and by his own breath of joviality. "Right this way, sir! It's a jolly ride, sir, with mince pies and hot toddy, if you care for such trifles!"

Mr Penfold inclined his head. "I am rather more concerned with spiritual refreshment," he said, "but I do not disdain bodily refreshment either." He smiled, as if he had discovered a kind of paradox, which indeed he had.

The train itself was a curious contrivance: a locomotive

painted green and gold, so polished it seemed as though it had been crafted by the hands of ancient monks - whose devotion, no doubt, was as much in the metalwork as in their prayers. Beyond the locomotive was a collection of carriages that smelled faintly of pine tar, wool, and something indefinably sweet, as if Christmas itself had secreted its essence into the varnish. As Mr Penfold clambered aboard, he felt a sudden, almost childlike elation: for he believed that a narrow-gauge railway was the perfect metaphor for the human soul - small, intricate, and easily diverted, yet capable of carrying a great weight if steered by faith.

He took his seat next to a window that framed a scene of frosted hills, twisted trees and the glimmer of a tarn so still that it seemed to reflect not merely the landscape, but the very shape of eternity. Beside him sat a lady reading a book with a concentration so profound that it seemed as though she were reading the very secrets of the universe, and a boy with a nose pressed to the glass, breathing fog onto it with the intensity of devotion.

"Are you enjoying your ride?" the lady asked, reluctantly glancing up from her book, not unkindly, but with a politeness that implied one must not ask too much of other people in such close quarters.

"I am," said Mr Penfold, "for I have always suspected that God sometimes prefers to speak in the hiss of a locomotive, the clatter of wheels and the faint smell of coal smoke."

The boy turned. "Really? He speaks to you through trains?"

"Indeed," said Mr Penfold. "Although I must admit that

sometimes He speaks through the puddles or through the awkwardness of small talk. But trains are more reliable."

The lady smiled. "Well, I suppose you have a point. They do carry you somewhere."

"Exactly!" said Mr Penfold, his voice suddenly rising in a whisper of revelation. "And that is, in essence, the vocation of all good men: to carry something, to go somewhere, to hold fast despite the curves and the gradients."

The train gave a cheerful cough and began to move. Mr Penfold leaned his head against the window and watched the winter landscape unfold. There was a kind of joy in the deliberate slowness, a kind of holiness in the steam curling upward into the cold air, as though even the smoke were praying.

He began to recount to himself the history of the line, which, as he imagined it, must have been established by saints in railwaymen's clothing, who understood that the proper way to honour God is to build something that lasts, yet brings pleasure. He suspected that the chief engineer had been a man of deep faith who had wept when the first spike was driven. Perhaps, he thought, God Himself had leaned over the plans and whispered a small encouragement.

As the train rattled on, Mr Penfold found himself embroiled in a kind of philosophical discourse with the boy, who had evidently appointed himself his pupil.

"Do you think trains go to Heaven?" the boy asked.

"I daresay," replied Mr Penfold. "At least, they go to places that remind us of Heaven. Do you notice the quiet of this valley? The way the snow softens the sound of the world? It is as though the hills themselves are kneeling."

The boy frowned. "But trains don't kneel."

"No," said Mr Penfold. "But men do, when they ride them wisely."

This, he felt, was a sufficiently mysterious and slightly terrifying answer. He allowed the boy to dwell upon it while he turned his attention to the scenery: a small bridge arching like a stone prayer over a rushing beck, a herd of sheep standing like grey statues upon the hillside and a distant village, where smoke rose from chimneys as though the houses themselves were sighing prayers of gratitude.

By the time the train had stopped at a tiny, picturesque station for refreshments, Mr Penfold had been swept up in a wave of contemplative delight. The station was adorned with holly, fairy lights and a nativity scene that seemed to wink at him with a conspiratorial jollity. He purchased a cup of mulled wine, which the ticket clerk assured him was blessed by the Christmas spirit, and sat upon a bench that creaked with age and moral certainty.

Mr Penfold mused aloud, as if the wind itself might listen: "There is something about these small stations that teaches humility. They are not grand, not imposing, yet they shelter us. They are proof that the divine can inhabit even the simplest forms."

Soon after, the conductor began to distribute mince pies.

"Do not rush your pie!" the conductor boomed, to no one

in particular. "A man who eats too quickly may miss the essence of the pastry, and perhaps the essence of life itself!"

Mr Penfold considered this wisdom carefully as he bit into a pastry that was indeed miraculous, a harmonious mixture of fruit, spice and something ineffably Christmassy. "The essence," he murmured, "is often hidden in the small things. And it is in the small things that God often dwells."

"You speak like a priest," said a man beside him, who had an ambitious moustache and eyes that suggested he had thought too deeply about the wrong things.

"I speak like a man who loves trains," said Mr Penfold, with the gentle gravity of someone who knows he is correct. "And the two are not so different. Both seek to carry their passengers safely, both follow a schedule of Divine Providence and both make one marvel at the curious balance of power and restraint."

The man nodded thoughtfully. "Well, I never thought of it that way. But I suppose it makes sense. Trains are like a choir, aren't they? Each one in its place, but no one ever quite knows what the conductor's up to."

As the train returned to motion, the boy beside him leaned closer and asked, "Do you think God likes narrow-gauge railways more than normal ones?"

Mr Penfold considered this with the kind of thoughtfulness usually reserved for philosophers or men with very large beards. "Yes," he said finally. "For narrow-gauge railways remind us that life is narrow. It is not the vastness of the track that teaches virtue, but the care with which we travel it. One cannot run a narrow-gauge railway recklessly -

though many do attempt it, usually when no one is looking. One must be attentive, prayerful, and ever-so-slightly amazed that the whole thing doesn't fall apart when you least expect it."

By now, the sun had begun to sink behind the fells, casting a golden light upon the valley. The train hissed and creaked and Mr Penfold leant back, feeling a deep, ineffable satisfaction. The world was at peace, or at least the world that mattered - the world of small, faithful gestures, of laughter, of coal smoke, of pious wonder.

As the train drew to its final stop, he stepped onto the platform and breathed in the winter air, which tasted of frost, burning coal, creosote, ash and eternity. He had seen the hills, he had conversed with the innocent and he had shared in a strange, joyous holiness that could only be found in a Christmas train ride.

And as he walked to his car, with the snow crunching softly underfoot, he felt certain of a great mystery: that perhaps the angels themselves had chosen the Lakelore Narrow Gauge Railway as their favourite passage, for it was narrow, yet true; humble, yet magnificent; fleeting, yet eternal. And he thought, with the kind of quiet triumph that only a devout and peculiar man can understand, that if this were a small miracle, it was still a miracle enough.

The Pruning of Roses

The first light of dawn had barely touched the cold earth when Benedict Campion stood in the garden, looking out at the rows of tangled rosebushes, their bare branches stretching toward the sky like skeletal hands. The faintest hint of frost clung to the leaves, glimmering like diamonds in the early morning haze. Benedict ran a gloved hand through his fair hair and over his arms, brushing off the very fine, almost invisible spiderwebs he had inadvertently walked through. The air cut against his cheeks, sharp and crisp, the way it always did in February. The world was quiet, still suspended between winter's cold grip and the promise of spring. As much as he loved this time of year, there was always a certain heaviness in it - a stillness that felt like waiting. The roses, in their dormant state, seemed to reflect that waiting, that expectation of something new coming. Something greater.

Benedict's sprawling collection of roses, his "palace of roses" as the family called it amongst themselves - climbers, ramblers, shrub and standard roses - took up almost the entire width and breadth of the garden. The palace of roses was intersected with a series of tiny, cobbled stone paths with a small, raised, two-tier stone fountain at the centre, now switched off for the cold winter months. The roses, dormant in their season of rest, stood as if frozen in time, their once vibrant blooms now nothing more than memories. Benedict's breath misted in the air as he let his gaze drift across the garden. It was his refuge, his place of solace - a sanctuary that had seen him through the darkest of times. And yet, for all the comfort it gave, it also spoke to him of the work yet to be done. It was time to prune.

He moved toward the first rosebush, its tangled vines like

old memories, curled around themselves, thick and unruly. Benedict had always loved these roses. For over a decade now, since the day he and Alice had moved into their thatched cottage on the outskirts of Stratford-upon-Avon, the ever-increasing collection of roses had been his joy, his kingdom. And yet, each year, they required the same patient attention - pruning away the dead growth, the twisted branches and any signs of disease.

This year, though, the task felt heavier than usual. Life had been harder than he liked to admit. His marriage, though grounded in love, had seen its trials: arguments that had felt too sharp, silences that had stretched too long. The financial pressures of his small business were mounting; money struggles had gnawed at him; and the burden of fatherhood, while a joy, had also been a responsibility that sometimes felt crushing. He thought of his own poor, dear father, whose health had deteriorated, slowly, then suddenly. The weight of that loss - of knowing that time was running out - had left Benedict feeling hollow. He hadn't known how to carry it, but there had been no choice but to keep going.

He knelt beside the first bush, gripping the secateurs, and snipped away the first small branch. There was something strangely satisfying in the motion, as though the simple act of cutting back the dead growth somehow made space for something new, something better. He couldn't help but draw the comparison between these rosebushes, the process of pruning and the struggles of his own life. Some of the pruning he'd endured over the past few years had been difficult to bear. There had been times when it seemed like God was slamming doors of opportunity closed for no apparent reason and then there were the times he felt, and still felt now, intensely sharp pain particularly now those business investments had gone wrong and his family were feeling the pinch.

But there was something deeper at work, something he hadn't fully understood until now. Just as these roses needed their deadwood removed, so too did his heart. It was painful. Necessary. And though he hadn't always seen it at the time, it had all been for a reason.

As the shears clicked against another branch, he thought of the passage from John 15:2: *"Every branch in me that beareth not fruit, he taketh away: and every branch that beareth fruit, he cleanseth it, that it may bear more fruit."*

Benedict paused. There it was. The secret of the garden, the secret of life itself: sometimes you need to be pruned before you can bear fruit. God didn't prune the dead things out of cruelty. He pruned them out of love, to create space for something better. God, Benedict realised, must love him a lot. Perhaps that's why the struggles of the past few years had felt so raw, so sharp at times - because God was at work, shaping him, preparing him for something greater.

As he worked, he found a strange kind of rhythm forming, a rhythm that mirrored his thoughts. He could see it now - the similarities between the roses and his life. In order for something beautiful to grow, there had to be something cut back. Some parts had to be torn away.

"Cut away the dead to make room for the living," he whispered sadly, almost to himself, as if the act of speaking the words might somehow help them settle in his heart.

And then, as if the garden itself had heard him, a distant sight caught his attention. He looked up, squinting into the blue sky. There, far off in the distance, three hot air balloons floated, their bright colours dotting the horizon like gentle whispers of joy. They drifted higher and higher, so serene against the backdrop of winter's last breath. It was a moment of beauty, of lightness, and it made him smile. Life, after all, was full of surprises.

As he returned to his task, he noticed something even stranger - a bumblebee. It was buzzing lazily around the rosemary plant, a late-winter-flowering variety whose tiny purple flowers were flourishing in full bloom despite the cold. Benedict stopped, astonished. It was too early for a bee to be out. It was still February. The poor creature must have been confused by the warmth of the mild winter.

He watched it for a long moment, as though in awe of its persistence. There was something in the bee's tenacity that spoke to him - its need to gather what it could, even in uncertain times. Maybe he, too, could learn to keep going in the face of things he couldn't control. Maybe there was still beauty to be found in the oddities of life.

"I've never been one for pruning," Alice had told him one winter afternoon, standing beside him in the garden, her arms wrapped tightly around her body against the cold. "It always feels like I'm cutting off pieces of something that could be useful."

Benedict had smiled, turning to her, his hands hugging a steaming mug of coffee. "But if you leave the dead parts, the rest of the plant can't thrive."

She'd looked at him, her brow furrowed, and for a moment, they'd both stood there in silence, watching the setting sun bathe the garden in its golden light. "I suppose you're right," she'd said, with a soft sigh. "Everything seems harder when you can't see the fruit yet. I can never be sure if I'm doing the right thing until I see it later."

Benedict had nodded, his gaze lingering on the roses, the blooms still far off in the distance. "Sometimes we're like that, aren't we? Waiting for the fruit without understanding the pruning process."

Now, in the stillness of the garden, those words returned to him with a clarity that he hadn't expected. Alice's voice echoed in his mind as he cut back yet another thick, gnarled branch. The thought of it gave him a strange sense of peace. The pain, the struggle - it was part of the plan. And just like the roses, there would be a season of new growth. There would be blossoms again, perhaps even more beautiful than before.

Benedict was startled by a soft chirp. He looked to his side and saw a robin hopping onto the nearby fence, puffed up against the cold. Its little feathers were round, almost cartoonishly so, as though it had stuffed itself with warmth for the winter. The robin cocked its head, watching Benedict with a knowing look, as if to say, *I see you, old friend.*

The robin had become a companion of sorts in the last year. It always appeared in the early mornings, when Benedict was working in the garden and hop about, so close that Benedict could hear its little feet tapping on the ground. Over time, he'd started to speak to it, his words not so much directed at the bird, but to the stillness of the garden around them.

"Good morning," Benedict said softly, his voice a little

hoarse. The robin chirped again, its round chest puffing out as it hopped closer, as if it were checking on him. He chuckled quietly. "Still here, eh? I've missed you too."

The robin seemed to agree, giving a small hop, then fluttering onto the rosebush beside him, as though observing his pruning with neighbourly curiosity.

The weight of Benedict's thoughts was interrupted when a sharp gust of wind blew through the garden, carrying with it the unmistakable scent of bacon. Benedict's stomach growled and he smiled. He could hear the distant sound of children's laughter - Pascal, Emily and Sebastian, cheerfully preparing breakfast together, by the sounds of it. It was a new enough responsibility for them to still be excited about it.

Alice, standing in the doorway, waved him in with a smile. In the quiet, Benedict took a deep breath and made his way back toward the cottage. Breakfast smelt mouth-wateringly delicious and, as he passed through the threshold of the little cottage, he felt a deep sense of peace settle into his bones.

The garden, the roses, the seasons - they had all been a reminder. That no matter how much pruning he endured, no matter the struggles he faced, God was working. And in the end, there would always be a season of blooming.

Spring

Panic at the Stables

It was one of those perfect, breezy mornings in Morecambe, the kind that made you realise this seaside town could be more of a secret paradise than anyone gave it credit for. The iconic stone jetty stretched out into the Bay, the clouds above were soft and welcoming, and the sweeping expanse of beach was as picturesque as any postcard. On days like this, even the seagulls seemed to be laughing at the idea of *not* being here.

Four friends stood on the pavement in front of *Bay View Stables*, shifting awkwardly in their ill-fitting riding helmets and stiff new riding boots they'd bought in a misguided attempt to look the part. Each of them looked like they were more likely to be running for cover than riding with grace, but nonetheless, they'd made it this far.

"I still think this was a terrible idea," muttered Steve, squinting at the stables like they might be harbouring *dangerous creatures*. "I mean… what's wrong with a nice, relaxing game of bingo?"

"Oh, please," Esther laughed, adjusting the oversized hat on her head. "It's a *beginner's hack*, Steve. A stroll down the beach on a pony. No big deal."

"Yeah, no big deal," Steve repeated, narrowing his eyes at the nearby horses. "Easy for you to say. You've actually ridden before."

Esther grimaced. "Once, when I was twelve, and I nearly fell off. But, like they say, *it's like riding a bike*."

"Or… it's like riding a bike *off a cliff*," muttered Brian, his fingers white as he gripped his jacket collar for dear life.

"Will you all just *shush* and enjoy Morecambe?" said Chloe, trying to sound more confident than she actually felt. Actually, she was so apprehensive about their forthcoming horse-riding session that her teeth were beginning to chatter. "Ook at this plashe," she said through visibly clenched teeth. The clenching of chattering teeth made it difficult to understand what she was saying. Chloe's words continued to come out in a muffled, inarticulate way. "The she's as att as a ann-ake, the horshesh are brilliant… and I'm shertain there's not a chansh of dying today."

Despite their nerves, the others giggled, not having really understood much of what Chloe had said through her clenched jaws - something about dying.

"That's how Sir Topham Hatt used to speak," observed Steve.

But a moment afterwards, they were looking at each other uncertainly again.

"Good morning, all!" came a bright voice from behind them.

It was too late to back out now.

They turned to find Karen, their instructor for the day, walking towards them like someone who had dealt with nervous beginners a *million* times and still had endless patience. She wore a *Bay View Stables* branded polo T-shirt and practical jodhpurs that screamed competence. But it was her smile that really put them at ease - it was warm, genuine and utterly unfazed by their collective nervousness.

"You must be the beginners," she said with a smile. "Don't worry, you're in safe hands. I'm Karen, and I'll be looking after you today."

"Er... *safe* hands, you say?" Steve muttered, already regretting his life choices.

Karen's smile widened. "That's right, my dears. I've been teaching people how to ride for *years* and I promise, you're in for a lovely time. Now, no one's going to be galloping off into the sunset today - unless it's in *slow motion*."

"I'll take slow motion," Brian said, looking towards the stables warily.

"And I'll take a miracle," Steve added.

Karen gave them a reassuring nod as she flipped through her clipboard. "So, it looks like you've all signed up for the... *People Terrified of Horse Riding* session, eh?"

The gang collectively winced.

Chloe, despite her best efforts, was on the verge of tears. Her knees were knocking so loudly that she could barely hear Karen's voice over the sound of her own panic. She tried to smile, but it looked more like an expression of sheer terror.

Karen raised an eyebrow as she glanced down at the clipboard. "Well, that's an interesting choice of wording," she said with a grin. "I think it might be a *bit* of a stretch to call you lot 'terrified.' You do all look like you're about to break into a sprint at any moment though, so I'd better keep my eye on you."

"No pressure, then," Steve said, with a laugh that sounded suspiciously like a duck in distress.

"I assure you, *no* pressure at all," Karen said, her tone calm and soothing. "We're just going to take things nice and easy. You're all going to love it, I promise. And if any of you end up in the sand, well, that's just a part of the learning process."

Chloe gulped, her smile faltering, as her right eye started to twitch of its own accord, like it had a mind of its own. She felt like she might faint.

Brian started doing a strange sort of nervous jig on the spot.

"Give over, Brian," hissed Esther, lightly slapping him on the back. "Stop mucking about."

"Right then," Karen said, ushering them toward the horses. "Let's meet your mounts."

The gang were led to the stables, each trying to appear like they belonged there, but looking like they were about to be dragged into an alien spaceship. One by one, the horses were brought out.

Steve was paired with a dignified grey mare named *Dusty*, whose every step seemed to say, *"Don't worry, I'll look after you. Maybe."*

Brian was given *Champ*, a horse so broad he looked like he could carry a small family on a *proper* adventure.

Chloe was paired with *Pineapple*, a horse whose name immediately made her nervous, but at least Pineapple had a sweet, if slightly bored, expression on her face.

And Esther? Esther got *Thunder*. A name that was both thrilling and terrifying, depending on how much you valued your life. Esther didn't seem to mind; she was the least nervous of the gang or at least acted that way.

"Now, remember," Karen said, walking them through the basics, "you'll want to keep your heels down, grip the reins gently, but firmly, and keep your back straight. Don't worry about the horse; just focus on keeping yourself balanced. And if you feel like you're going to fall, just *breathe* and I'll be right there."

Chloe's knees wobbled as she mounted Pineapple, but she did as Karen had said. "Heels down, shoulders back, breathe…" she repeated under her breath, wondering for the hundredth time why she had ever agreed to do this. And was it even *normal* to be in a friendship group where they were ALL terrified of horses? She'd never heard of that before.

Karen was beside her in an instant, sensing the nerves. "You're doing wonderfully, Chloe," she said kindly, placing a gentle hand on her shoulder. "Pineapple's a gentle one, she'll take care of you. And if anything *does* happen, just trust me - I've got you."

"Thanks," Chloe said, managing a watery smile. "I'm… I'm fine. Totally fine."

"Good! That's the spirit," Karen cheered. "You'll feel much

better once we start moving. And I promise, no surprise galloping. You're not here for *the Grand National*, just a peaceful stroll along the beach."

Esther's confidence was misplaced. She launched from the mounting block with what was supposed to be a dramatic hair flip that didn't quite work whilst wearing a riding helmet. Then, instead of landing gracefully, she flew over *Thunder*'s back, missing it altogether, and crashed into a hay bale. Red-faced with embarrassment, Esther brushed herself off and tiptoed round to the mounting block to try again. Luckily, nobody had noticed because everyone else was focusing on assisting Steve, who, nearly frozen in his fear, found he could only shuffle forward an inch or two at a time, sobbing loudly, "That's not a horse, it's a *hearse*," several times as he went. "A *hearse!*"

At long last, all of the gang were safely mounted upon their trusty steeds. Undaunted, Karen turned to the group, giving them all the same steady, reassuring smile. "Ready for your adventure? There's no rush, just follow me and we'll keep it nice and easy."

The gang nodded reluctantly, but as the horses plodded slowly forwards, Chloe let out a shriek, Steve's face blanched and Brian cried out desperately, "I can do all things in him that strengtheneth me!" believing these might well be his last ever words.

Amid the chaos, Chloe desperately gasped aloud, "My Will - Brian - my Last Will and Testament! If anything happens to me, remember I told you where to find it. Remember!"

"Can't - focus - on - that - at - moment," wheezed Brian, his voice unnaturally dry as he gripped the reins in his white-knuckled hands and shut his eyes tightly.

However, when they set off down the quiet lane towards the beach, something amazing happened. Karen's calm presence, combined with the stunning views of Morecambe Bay and the steady, sturdy amble of the horses, started to melt their fears.

The sea stretched out before them, the waves lapping gently at the shore. The horses walked in sync, their hooves leaving prints in the soft sand as the sun began to warm the air.

"I could get used to this," Esther said, with a nervous smile, the wind catching her hair. "The amazing views, the sound of the waves… This is the most beautiful coast in the world."

"I'm still trying to figure out why anyone would want to sit on a horse," Steve said, still clinging to Dusty like it was the last thing keeping him from being swept away. "But yeah, the view's nice."

"I'm proud of you lot," Karen called back. "You're all doing *great*. Just a little further and then we'll turn back. You'll be amazed how much you've improved by the end of the session."

Chloe, whose legs still felt like jelly, gave her a grateful smile. "Thanks, Karen… You're really, really good at this."

"I just love horses," Karen replied with a wink. "And I love seeing people face their fears and come out the other side grinning like mad."

As they continued down the beach, each of them began to settle into the rhythm of the ride, even if they were still more shaky than graceful. Dusty's steady pace and Pineapple's calm demeanour made them feel like they weren't about to crash into the sea at any moment.

By the time they returned to the stables, the friends were tired, but also... triumphant. They had survived the hack. They had faced their fears. And maybe, just maybe, they were ready to do it again - *tomorrow*. Or maybe not - actually, almost certainly never again.

"Do you know what?" said Esther, still grinning. "That was brilliant! Best idea we've ever had."

"I'm going back to bingo next time," Steve said, breathless. "Much less *terrifying*."

But the smile on Chloe's face said it all: *maybe* next time, she wouldn't be *quite* as terrified.

Karen, who had overheard their conversation, smiled softly and said, "You all did brilliantly today, truly. You faced your fears and didn't let them stop you. And that's something worth celebrating."

Chloe nodded, a Bible verse she had read before setting out this morning echoing in her mind:

'Fear thou not, for I am with thee; be not dismayed, for I am thy God; I will strengthen thee; yea, I will help thee; yea I will uphold thee with the right hand of my righteousness." - Isaiah 41:10

The verse felt like it had been written just for her in that moment - when fear threatened to keep her from stepping out of her comfort zone, she had been reminded that God's strength was always there to carry her through. She wasn't alone.

Karen had been a wonderful guide on the journey, but in the end, it was Chloe's faith and trust that had truly helped her find the courage to face her fear and step forward.

"I think I might take on *more than just horses* next time," Chloe whispered to herself, smiling, feeling ready for whatever came next.

The friends hugged each other with pride and relief. It was one thing to admit to being afraid of something, but another thing altogether for them to have faced that fear as one.

As they walked towards the promenade for some freshly made doughnuts and another look out to sea, Brian, who had been quiet, piped up, "It's not just horse riding, you know. I've always been scared of sky-diving too," he began, "Maybe next time, we can all -"

"NOOOO!" yelled the rest of the gang in unison.

"Let's stick to bingo for now," said Steve, soothingly, then with an irrepressible twinkle in his eye, he began mimicking the funny, nervous jigging movements Brian had made earlier.

"Oh, and nice flight over your horse, Peter Pan," chortled Brian, his eyes sparkling mischievously at Esther. And she'd thought that no one had seen!

"That was just my… re-*hearse*-al," Esther punned back, glancing cheekily at Steve.

"Well, where there's a *Will*, there's a way, eh Chloe?" guffawed Steve.

The sound of the gang's good-natured and raucous laughter rang out as they entered the delicious-smelling Promenade Cafe.

The Garden Meeting

It was the first Sunday in March, and the air still had a bite to it - a quiet kind of cold that lingered despite the gentle nudges of spring. Outside, in the slanting light that stretched across the hedgerows and grazed the tips of the beeches lining the lane, crocuses stood like little votive candles in the grass, and the first daffodils had begun to trumpet shyly along the verge. Yellow pompom flowers adorned the kerria shrub and the forsythias were also garlanded with gold. The front wall of Bluebell Cottage was threaded with the bare, twisting limbs of a wisteria that - come May - would unfurl a spectacular cascade of dreamy purple blooms around the windows and front door.

Inside Bluebell Cottage - a creamy Cotswold-stone house - set on the gently rising outskirts of Wheatley, Oxfordshire, where bridleways dip between fields of early wheat and the lanes still echo with traces of the old coaching road - the Hill family, having returned home from Mass and shared a Sunday roast together, had gathered round the worn pine table in their kitchen in the afternoon, wrapped in the kind of warmth that only kettle steam and familial chatter can provide.

Laura Hill poured a second pot of tea and her husband, George, who still had a smear of compost beneath one fingernail from re-potting the hydrangeas, passed around a plate of warm fruit scones, all buttery and crumbling.

"Lent starts next week, so enjoy these while you can!" chuckled Granny Eileen who lived in the annex and kept the family well-supplied with mouthwatering home-baked buns and breads.

Spread across the table were half a dozen well-thumbed seed catalogues, a pile of garden magazines and books, and several scraps of graph paper bearing hopeful diagrams in pencil.

"All right, team," Laura said, tugging her cardigan closer. "The garden is a blank canvas and we are the artists. Let's decide what goes where before the frost lifts for good."

Eight-year-old Rosie, who had fashioned herself a crown from winding green stems and the last of the snowdrops from their own garden, bounced on her chair. "I want a pizza garden!" she declared with the sort of conviction only a child could muster. "Like a real pizza, round and cut into slices - one slice for tomatoes, one for basil, one for oregano, and maybe one for peppers!"

"Wow!" chuckled George, impressed. "Will it be stone-baked, too?"

Rosie grinned. "I was thinking we could use the stones from the old path, the ones in the shed. Make the slices that way. It'll look just like a real pizza, Dad, I promise!"

"Rosie, that's a brilliant idea," Laura said, already reaching for the planner. "We could position it near the back wall - south-facing. It'll get sun all day, come June. Good for the tomatoes."

Across the table, ten-year-old Isaac, thoughtful as always, tapped a pencil against his lip. "I want a rockery," he said. "Something with alpines and gravel, and maybe some logs and moss. Like the ones we saw at the Botanic Garden, last Summer holiday."

"Oh yes, at the Oxford Botanic Garden," enthused Laura. "And, in fact, at Waterperry Gardens too - do you remember we saw the National Collections they have of some Alpine plants? I remember how interested you were in them when we visited."

Isaac nodded. "They had saxifrages and those little sedums that look like green jellybeans. And the lizards like it warm. Maybe we'll get slow worms again."

"There's plenty of stone left over from when we fixed the wall," George mused. "We could stack it near the side gate, under the pear tree. Not ideal for fruit, but perfect for your micro-mountain, Isaac."

Laura looked from Isaac to Rosie, her eyes full of affection and something close to awe.

"Wowzers," she gasped, almost laughing with delight. "You two! These ideas are amazing - I'm genuinely impressed. You're my two gardening geniuses!"

Grinning in agreement, George gave a low whistle and leaned back in his chair.

"I've seen professionals come up with less imaginative plans," he said. "Rosie, that pizza garden's inspired. And Isaac, I'd love to help you build that rockery - proper little nature reserve, that'll be."

Granny Eileen, who'd been quietly enjoying her second scone, gave an approving nod. "Well, I think it's marvellous," she said, smiling at them both. "When I was your age, I'd have given anything to plan my own little patch. You've both got such imagination. I'd say the Chelsea

Flower Show had better watch its back."

Granny paused for a moment, then reached for her teacup and, giving a thoughtful little hum, glanced toward the window, where the garden lay waiting under the pale sky.

"As for me," she added, "I should like a cutting garden. Something by the shed. Dahlias, cosmos, cornflowers. I can grow them for the church flower rota and for the house."

They all turned to look at her, warmed by the thought. She rarely asked for anything.

"Done," said Laura, scribbling it in. "Cut flowers for Granny. Pizza garden for Rosie. Rockery for Isaac."

"And us?" George asked, eyebrow raised.

"Vegetables, of course," she said. "Your runner beans and my carrots - and courgettes, if we can keep the slugs off this year."

Isaac smirked. "You'll need an army of frogs."

"Maybe we'll build a pond next year," said George, pretending to note it on his napkin. "Phase two."

Outside, a gust of wind sent the wind chimes on the porch into a soft, metallic lullaby. Inside, the kettle whistled again. Rosie leapt up to feed the cat; Isaac was already leafing through a magazine on alpine soil; and George began sketching the curved lines of Rosie's pizza garden on the back of an envelope.

And so, it was decided. A family garden sown, not by

perfection, but by personality. A little bit wild, a little bit charming. Much like the family themselves.

Soon the frost would lift, the soil would be turned and the days would lengthen. But, for now, in their kitchen in Oxfordshire, with steam on the windows and muddy boots by the door, everything felt exactly as it should.

The Cove and the Canvas

The early morning mist clung gently to the folds of the Cornish cliffs like an old, familiar shawl. The air was silver and soft, threaded with salt and the distant cry of gulls. Down a narrow, hedge-lined lane where the earth smelled of rain and wild thyme, a woman walked with slow determination. She was burdened, not just by the weight of the wooden easel strapped awkwardly to her back or the clattering of paint tubes in the canvas satchel, but by the tremble of something far deeper: hope, old and aching, almost forgotten.

Her name was Monica Walker and she was sixty-three years old. Never once in her life had she painted, but this morning - this peculiar, sacred morning - she had risen before the sun and known, with a clarity rare and tender, that she must go to the sea.

The path curved gently downhill, the brambles brushing her skirt, the dew glistening like tiny diamonds across the gorse. Her boots sank slightly into the damp soil, but she paid it no heed. To the left, a field of barley rippled like a golden sea, alive with morning light; to the right, granite outcrops sat squat and eternal, softened by lichen and the kiss of centuries. In the near distance, beyond the knotted hedgerows and sheep-dotted meadows, the sea revealed itself - first a hint, then a glimmer, then a glorious sweep of blue and silver, framed by rugged headlands like open arms.

She reached the clifftop just as the sun broke through, golden and triumphant. Below her, the cove lay quiet, the tide obediently out, revealing dark rocks and creamy sand streaked with the imprint of gulls' feet. The sea breathed gently against the land, each wave folding into itself with a whisper. A handful of boats bobbed far out on the glinting expanse and, above it all, the sky arched wide and infinitely kind.

Monica found a patch of level ground not far from the edge and began to set up. Her fingers fumbled with the easel, the unfamiliar joints and hinges making her mutter under her breath. The wind lifted her grey hair and flung it playfully into her face. She laughed, softly, nervously.

"No idea what I'm doing," she murmured to the horizon.

In truth, she didn't. The brushes were still in their plastic wrappers, the tubes of paint uncreased. Yet something within her burned with longing - not for perfection, not even for beauty, but for expression, for obedience to a call she had ignored for decades. She'd spent her life in offices and kitchens, raising children, tending a husband now long passed, always too busy, too practical, too tired.

Now there was no one watching, no one needing. Just her, the paints and this living masterpiece of coast and light and wind.

Still, fear coiled in her belly like a cold eel. What if someone came down the path and saw her? What if they asked her what she was painting and she had no answer? What if they looked at her canvas and smiled kindly - *too* kindly? Or worse, laughed?

She sat, hands trembling slightly, the brush hovering above the white. The emptiness of the canvas frightened her almost as much as the fullness of her heart.

She whispered a prayer. "Lord, be with me. Not because

I'm clever or good at this, but because You made the sea, and You made me, and You gave me this day."

Then, with a breath as deep as the ocean itself, she dipped the brush into blue.

The first stroke was hesitant, wavering. The second bolder. Soon, colours began to emerge, awkward and childlike, but earnest. The sea was too dark, the cliff too high, the sky not quite right - but she painted with her whole heart, as if the act itself was worship. She heard no footsteps, saw no strangers, only the ever-changing sea, the wheeling birds, the wild freedom of it all.

She lost track of time. The light shifted, golden to white to honeyed once more, and still she painted. Not well, perhaps. But truly.

And in that quiet cove, a woman who had once believed her purpose had passed her by, found it at last - not in success, not in skill, but in surrender. The painting was not magnificent. But it was hers, and it was real.

As she packed her things and looked once more at the view - the cliffs rugged with age, the sea speaking in its ancient tongue, the sky endless above - Monica smiled, a tear tracing her cheek.

A verse came to her, one she hadn't thought of in years:

"Delight thyself also in (the Lord); and he will give thee the desires of thy heart." - Psalm 37:4

Not the applause of others. Not the neatness of skill. But the deep, hidden desire planted long ago by the very One who made the sea. And brought her, finally, to see it not just with her eyes - but with her soul.

The Return of the Merry Maids
by an author who knows Sherwood's secrets

Mabel Cooper and Edna Green had been best friends since the Blitz, when they shared an Anderson shelter, a battered tin of condensed milk and a lifelong sense of mischief. Now, at the grand age of eighty-three, they found themselves on a train to Nottinghamshire, chattering like girls as the rolling green hills of Robin Hood's country flickered by the window.

"Do you think the Major Oak remembers us?" Edna asked, eyes twinkling beneath a hat that looked suspiciously like it belonged on a prize-winning pig at the county fair.

"I hope not," Mabel replied. "I carved 'M loves T' on it in 1953. Poor Thomas. He never stood a chance."

Edna gasped, "You never did! No wonder they've cordoned it off nowadays."

Their carriage rattled to a stop, and soon they were stepping off the platform into the fresh woodland air of Sherwood Forest - a place that, in their childhood, had seemed as endless and enchanted as Heaven itself. The path to the Major Oak twisted beneath archways of ancient oaks and Scots pines. Ferns curled like green fiddleheads along the forest floor, and the scent of pine needles and bluebells filled their lungs.

As they walked, they passed towering Norway spruce trees and shy robins flitting through slivers of light that rained down as if Heaven were shaking out its pockets. A squirrel stopped on a branch to stare at the two old ladies with something close to disbelief.

"Do you think that's one of Robin's men reincarnated?" Edna asked solemnly, nodding at the squirrel.

"If it were a red squirrel, then perhaps I might say so," retorted Mabel, "but those grey ones," Here, she shuddered. "Well, they're no better than the wicked Sheriff of Nottingham's men, I tell you - outlawing and hounding down all the good red squirrels till there's practically none of them left."

Here Mabel made as if to shake her walking stick at the squirrel.

"Now, Mabel, remember that arm of yours," broke in Edna. "Last time you got carried away threatening the wildlife, we spent six hours in A&E and you missed Mass."

"I wasn't threatening, I was gesturing with righteous indignation," Mabel sniffed, adjusting her walking stick like it was a sword from King Richard's own armoury. "And I maintain that pheasant had it coming."

Edna rolled her eyes. "It was a wooden carving outside the visitor centre."

"A very menacing carving, if I may say so."

The squirrel, now perched with one paw suspiciously close to its tiny chest, blinked at them.

"Look at it, Edna. Mark my words, it's planning something. Probably been sent by the council to spy on us pensioners."

"Oh yes," said Edna drily, "MI6's top rodent operative,

codename *Nutcracker*."

They stood there for a moment, giggling, the forest echoing with birdcall and merriment.

"Well, I'd best save my energy, I suppose," sighed Mabel wryly. "After all, we've got three miles, two sandwiches, and one dodgy hip between us."

"Come on," said Edna, smiling and linking arms with her friend. "Let's go and find that oak. You've got a decades-old act of tree vandalism to confess."

"And I've got a pinecone stuck in my shoe."

"And we call this a holiday."

"Better than a coach trip to Bognor Regis," said Mabel, a mischievous glint in her eye that Edna, for now, missed.

"Now, you know I love Bognor, Mabel, it's just that coach trip was far too long and - what's more - that dreadful smell -" Edna began, only to pause mid-sentence.

Mabel was walking beside her, lips twitching in perfect time, mouthing every familiar word - including the bit Edna hadn't even said yet.

Edna stopped and squinted at her, then burst into a wheezy chuckle. "Oh, you menace. You've memorised my entire Bognor rant!"

"I could perform it on the pier," Mabel replied sweetly.

"You'll pay for that, Mabel Cooper. Mark my words."

"And yet, 'totally worth it' - as the youngsters say."

And with that, the two old ladies tottered deeper into the emerald pavilion of Sherwood, laughing like girls who had never really left.

The squirrel, meanwhile, blinked slowly and scampered away, presumably to file a report titled *Subjects: Elderly, Armed, Slightly Unstable. Proceed with Caution.*

They reached the Major Oak, its vast, hollow trunk propped up by iron rods like a grand old man leaning on his walking stick. Sunlight streamed through leaves so green they seemed almost unreal, dappling the ground with shifting patterns of emerald and gold.

A sudden breeze stirred the canopy, whispering through the leaves. Mabel looked up. "I remember Mum telling us to be quiet here, may she rest in peace. She said it was holy ground, because God made the trees to show His strength."

Edna nodded. "Funny, isn't it? All these years, and it still feels… bigger than us. Like God's here, hiding just out of sight."

They stood hand in hand, their wrinkles catching the sun, feeling small and young again. Then, because they were who they were, they began to giggle. A high, bubbling giggle that startled a family of red deer grazing nearby and earned them scandalised looks from a passing group of serious hikers.

"We're going to get thrown out of Sherwood Forest," Edna wheezed.

"Imagine explaining that to Father Oliver," Mabel replied, wiping tears of laughter from her cheeks.

They sat down on a bench within sight of the mighty oak and shared a flask of tea that tasted faintly of metal. Overhead, a woodpecker drummed its tattoo against a branch. Mabel pointed it out, and they fell silent again, marvelling at how alive the forest felt - how each rustle, each call of a blackbird, each sigh of wind reminded them of the quiet joy and grandeur God had woven into His creation.

They prayed together, a few simple words for their children and grandchildren, and thanked God for letting them live long enough to return to this place. In that dappled light, Sherwood was no longer a distant memory but a living testament: that love, faith, and friendship can last longer than even the oldest oak.

And when they finally stood, knees creaking, they linked arms and shuffled back along the path - past early foxgloves nodding in the breeze, past sunlight spilling like honey on the forest floor - chattering of Sunday roasts and the chance of rain, their hearts lighter than they'd been in years.

Heart of Dartmoor

It was the second Tuesday of April and Dartmoor - our Dartmoor, wide and wind-washed and stubbornly alive - had decided that spring had officially begun.

There had been a few false starts, of course. Dartmoor does not move quickly in these matters. A few hesitant buds in March. A brief afternoon of sunshine that was chased away by a week of sleet. But now, in the Easter Octave, it was as though the entire moor had woken with a yawn and a stretch, and remembered it had flowers to grow.

The heather hadn't yet bloomed, but the gorse had taken the lead, lighting up the hills in vivid waves of gold, as though God had tipped over a bowl of sunshine.

I had taken the train to Newton Abbot the week before and thence by borrowed bicycle, rucksack flapping behind me like a sail. I was on my way to visit the little village of Fernycombe, tucked high up on the edge of the moor, not far from Widecombe-in-the-Moor. As it turned out, Fernycombe was the sort of place you stumbled upon by accident and remembered for the rest of your life.

My old friend Father Hugh, the parish priest at *Our Lady of the Tors*, had written last year to say I ought to come and see the parish in springtime.

"It does something to the soul," he'd said in his letter, "that even my most well-rehearsed sermons can't manage. We've just finished our Divine Mercy devotions - Mass, confessions, the Chaplet, the lot - and the moor is humming with grace."

The road to Fernycombe curled through the rising hills like a question mark and, as I cycled on, the wind's cool touch brushed my cheeks, already flushed with the effort. With each breath, Dartmoor's air filled my lungs, crisp and invigorating, carrying the faint scent of bracken and sheep's wool and drawing me into the heart of the moor, as though the land itself were breathing with me.

Skylarks sang high above, invisible in the blue, joined by the soft, staccato chirrup of stonechats hidden in the gorse. In the distance, the tors rose up - not as dramatic as mountains, perhaps, but older, wiser, somehow, and more trustworthy.

There were lambs in the fields. I stopped to watch two of them trying to climb a rock while their mother looked on, chewing cud in a mood that seemed equal parts pride and resignation.

Eventually, after a stiff climb, I arrived at the village. A cluster of stone cottages, a post box, a bakery with excellent pasties and at the centre of it all, *Our Lady of the Tors* - a modest granite church with a low tower and stained glass that caught the sun like a smile.

Father Hugh greeted me outside the presbytery, his cassock slightly askew and his eyes twinkling in the way of those who know where all the biscuits are kept.

"You made it," he said. "Come in and I'll put the kettle on. There's a fire and Mrs Pengelly's made saffron buns."

Now, let it be said plainly: I have never known a more

peaceful three days.

The people of Fernycombe live close to the land and their hearts are shaped by the seasons. They speak kindly, listen well and give you the sense that Heaven is never very far away. Fernycombe moves at its own pace. Even the red grouse, their feathers ruffled by the wind, take their time, calling out their plaintive song from the heather, as if they, too, know there's no need to hurry.

Each morning, I joined Father Hugh for Mass in the little church, the candles flickering gently, the peace full, not of silence, but of *life* - the murmur of children, a baby's cry, the rustle of missals, all the sounds singing together the Church's joy. Sunlight streamed through the windows, warming the pale yellow walls with a gentle glow. On the second day, the village children brought daffodils to place by the altar and the effect was such that I caught myself blinking back tears for no good reason at all.

On the Friday, we took a walk up towards Haytor, following an old sheep path that threaded between gorse and granite, the rough surfaces of the ancient stones cool and moss-dappled beneath my fingertips. We had just rounded a slope when I saw them - four ponies, standing motionless among the rocks as if they'd grown from the moor itself. Their coats were rough and thick, the colour of peat and smoke, their manes tangled by the wind. I could hear the slow pull of their breath and the faint scuff of their hooves on the wet turf. They smelled of rain and old grass. None of them looked at us. They simply existed, quietly, with the self-assurance of something that had always belonged. I held my breath, as if speaking might break whatever spell held them there.

"Servant of God John Bradburne lived as a hermit in a cave somewhere near here," Father Hugh told me as we continued on our way. "Before he went to Zimbabwe. No one's quite certain exactly where, but I like to think that, in some small way, I'm treading the same paths he once wandered."

The breeze lifted the bracken and the tors stood in the distance, solemn and enigmatic. They seemed to welcome me, in a way I couldn't quite understand, as if the land had always known my name, even though I had never set foot here before. I found myself wondering if Father Hugh had ever felt the same.

As we walked, he spoke of his parishioners - the quiet heroism of the young mother who, besides singing in the choir, cared devotedly for her father; the elderly gentleman who, rain or shine, brought in the church flowers every Saturday, wrapped in damp cloths from his greenhouse.

"It's rarely the loud things," he said, stopping to admire a bank of wild violets. "Often it's what looks small from the outside - but costs a person everything. That's where grace lands, I think."

We sat for a while on a granite outcrop just below the tor, the stone still warm from the sun. A spring breeze brushed my cheek, gentle yet insistent, as though urging me to listen to the land around me. From high up there, the land seemed to unfold endlessly - rolling heather and bracken giving way to the long, broken spine of the moor. In the near distance, the dark combes dipped and folded into one another like the backs of sleeping animals. Far off, I thought I could just make out the glint of the sea beyond

Teignmouth, where the land gives up and lets the water in. Overhead, the clouds moved slowly, like thoughtful pilgrims.

"Do you know what I love about Dartmoor?" said Fr Hugh, his voice gently interrupting my thoughts.

I gave him an encouraging nod.

"It's not just the beauty of it," he continued, "though, of course, there's that. It's the honesty. The moor doesn't pretend to be anything it's not. It's bare and it's open. It's not always comfortable. But it's never false. You can't be vain on Dartmoor, or clever. You can only be... grateful."

We sat in silence, and I understood exactly what he meant.

The parish Divine Mercy picnic, held on the Sunday afternoon, was a joyful affair.

That morning, the whole village had gathered for Divine Mercy Sunday. Confessions were heard - Father Hugh had brought in two other priests to assist - and then came Holy Mass, followed by the Divine Mercy Chaplet. The prayer rose up, a chorus of full hearts and radiant joy. Young children ran about, their laughter mingling with the sound of prayer. A woman with learning disabilities made joyful, unrestrained sounds, and a teenage boy, also with learning disabilities, danced freely in the aisle, praising God in the way that was uniquely his. There was not a glance of judgment, not a whispered disapproval - just love. To me, it felt like Paradise. An unknown weight lifted from my heart and, in this moment, eternity wasn't some far-off dream, but a living, embracing Presence, just within reach.

We made our way, after Mass, to the meadow below the village, where the trees were bright with new leaves and the cow parsley danced in the breeze. A red and white banner bearing the words *Jesus, I trust in You* hung from the hawthorn branches, tenderly billowing, while the soft wind carried the comforting aromas of baking and warm jam from the tables, sweeping through my senses and settling into my rumbling stomach.

The Divine Mercy cream tea was, by all accounts, a triumph. The children had Divine Mercy ice cream sundaes, with red strawberry sauce and white whipped cream and the adults tucked into scones topped with red jam and a generous dollop of thick Devon clotted cream - "the colours of mercy made edible," as Mrs Pengelly put it. There were also sausage rolls, potato salad, gooseberry tart and a Victoria sponge so perfectly risen it drew appreciative murmurs.

The children ran about laughing, hunting for chocolate eggs left behind by an enthusiastic catechist, and Father Hugh - normally a slow-moving figure of quiet dignity - was found halfway up a tree, attempting to retrieve a football with a crook borrowed from a shepherd.

There was no programme, no speeches. Just friendship, food, faith and the kind of happiness that comes when everyone knows they are loved and have a place.

At the end, a softly-spoken young woman from the parish began to sing a final Chaplet beneath the trees and, one by one, the rest of us joined her - our voices rising gently and confidently, mingling with birdsong and the soft rustle of the wind.

That night, walking back through the dusk, I paused on the edge of the moor.

The air was still. The gorse was glowing faintly gold, even in the twilight. In the distance, the tors stood quiet and sure, rising from the moor like old bones in the earth. A few stars had appeared and one could just hear the far-off bleat of a lamb.

And I thought of the children and their laughter, of Mass alive with love and praise, of the daffodils by the altar, and the soft, clear voices singing the Chaplet beneath the hawthorn trees.

God is not far off in places like this. He walks the lanes, I think. He stops to admire the primroses.

And I, who had come to Dartmoor for nothing more than rest and the company of an old friend, began to wonder if, in doing so, God had quietly opened a door - one that led, almost without my noticing, to the next part of life's journey. The moor had opened something in me. Or perhaps I had simply opened to it.

I returned to the city the next day. The trees there were greening, the air softening. Spring had arrived even in the streets and the stone. But a part of my heart stayed up on Dartmoor, among the tors and the heather, where the gorse flames like gold and the skies stretch wide and holy.

I shall go back soon, I think.
In truth, my heart will not rest until I do.

Summer

Petals and Providence

The Wilted Life

On the seventh floor of a faceless concrete office block, buried deep in the centre of a city whose breath smelled faintly of wet asphalt and exhaust fumes, Eleanor Grace Lockhart sat beneath the soul-bleaching flicker of fluorescent lights. The ticking of the wall clock mimicked the slow, persistent drip of water against stone - not enough to flood, but enough to wear something down.

Her hands, capable and once joyful, tapped dull letters into duller spreadsheets. Her soul, made for beauty and fragrance and morning dew, sagged like a poppy bowed in heavy rain.

Eleanor had once dreamt of doing something meaningful - something that left the world better than it found it. But dreams are quiet things and the world, with its bills and expectations and polite small talk about weekend plans, is so very loud.

It wasn't that she disliked work. It was just that it didn't love her back.

Her only solace lay forty miles away, just past the church with the bell that rang like a hymn: There, in the garden she'd tended for two years, peace waited - tucked behind her modest, whitewashed stone cottage where roses climbed the walls like praises rising to Heaven.

There, in rich soil and sun-warmed beds, her real life bloomed.

The Garden of Small Beginnings

Each evening, Eleanor would escape the office like a bird loosed from a too-small cage, kick off her shoes the moment she stepped over the threshold, and pull on her wellingtons. She would wander among the herbs and flowering shrubs like Adam in Eden before the fall, hands brushing against lavender, thyme, calendula, lemon balm and, her favourite - chamomile.

The chamomile was always faithful. It grew in soft golden mounds, smelling of apples and sunlight. She would sit beside it, her Bible open in her lap, reading aloud the Psalms to the bees.

(The Lord) is gracious, and merciful; Slow to anger, and of great lovingkindness. - Psalm 145:8

The garden grew. And so did she.

One Saturday morning, as mist lifted like a veil from the grass, she plucked a bundle of chamomile and thought, *I wonder if I could do something more with this.*

It began with soap - nothing grand, only a few bars. She researched, cautiously at first, scribbling down notes from blogs and books, experimenting with lye and oils. Her kitchen smelled of olive oil and honey, lemon zest and eucalyptus. When she unmoulded the first bar and cut it into smooth, creamy slices, it felt like slicing through light itself.

She gave a few bars away - to Maud from church, to the widower next door, to her sister's friend who worked at the school. Their response was universal: *"This is lovely. Truly lovely. You should sell it."*

A Hopeful Venture

There are few moments in a quiet life more thrilling than choosing to believe in the seed of a dream.

Eleanor applied for her legal certifications, half-expecting to be told she'd missed something crucial. But everything passed.

She invested her modest savings into better moulds, richer oils and natural pigments the colours of earth and herb and dusk. Peppermint that tingled like morning light. Tea tree sharp as flint. Rosehip and oatmeal, soft as remembered skin. Clary sage. Geranium. She taught herself the quiet science of shampoo bars, then conditioner bars, each batch infused with patience and prayer. On stormy nights, with the cat curled warm against her lap and Psalm 23 murmured under her breath, she designed packaging by candlelight - hand-drawn, hand-cut, hand-tied.

And then came the farmers and crafts markets.

Eleanor's first ever stall was at the Shambles Market in York's historic 'olde worlde' city centre - a vibrant open-air market tucked just behind The Shambles. York's famous medieval street was lined with crooked timber-framed buildings that leaned in close like old friends sharing secrets. Stone archways opened onto cobbled courtyards and bunting hung from shopfront to lamppost in cheerful strands.

Her stall was small - a trestle table covered with linen, sprigs of lavender scattered among the baskets and handstamped labels tied with twine. She called her brand *Grace Made*.

Eleanor stood behind her stall, heart fluttering like a robin in the hedge, wearing a smile that was half hope and half prayer.

And they came.

People stopped. Picked up the bars. Breathed deeply. Smiled. Bought. By noon, her chamomile soap had sold out. By one-thirty, there was nothing left but the sign. The elderly lady from the bakery bought four bars and said, *"It reminds me of my mother's hands."*

The Unfolding

That night, Eleanor sat at her kitchen table with a cup of mint tea and stared at the empty soap baskets in astonishment.

She opened her Bible to Psalm 126: *"They that sow in tears shall reap in joy."*

She wept - not in sorrow, but in overwhelming joy that something had shifted, that she had stepped into her true path. God, in His quiet mercy, had not forgotten her.

Soon, a simple website was launched. Orders came in - first a trickle, then a stream. Word spread, quietly, but with conviction. A blogger featured her shop. A deacon's wife recommended her to a retreat centre in the Lake District. Customers sent messages like, *"This soap healed more than my skin,"* and *"Thank you for making something so beautiful."*

She hired her cousin part-time. Then a retired chemist from

church offered to help her with product development. Her days were full of fragrances and formulas, her evenings of fulfilment and emails. And still, the garden bloomed.

Leaving Egypt

Eighteen months after that first market stall, Eleanor walked out of the office building for the last time.

She left behind the spreadsheets, sighing lifts and lukewarm coffee, and stepped into her new calling - a life where hands make, where hearts listen, where work is worship.

On the morning of her freedom, she rose early, knelt in the dew-wet grass of her garden and gave thanks.

"Lord, I didn't know You were planting something in me all along. I only thought I was planting flowers."

She had learned, as the seasons taught her, that small things grow. That faith, like chamomile, flourishes when given light and patience. That obedience often begins with dirt under fingernails and the courage to begin again.

A Future of Fragrance

Today, *Grace Made* ships products across Great Britain. A handwritten verse accompanies each parcel. Eleanor often walks through the market with her little notepad, talking to customers who have become friends, offering samples to curious passers-by.

Her hands are strong now - scrubbed clean with the work of honest making. Her eyes are bright, reflecting something that doesn't dim.

She meets each day with the same prayer she murmured over her garden:

"Lord, bless the work of my hands. Let it glorify You."

And though her little whitewashed cottage is still modest, her heart sings in cathedral tones.

Epilogue: The Last Word

In the living room, beside a jug of wildflowers, sits a framed verse in neat calligraphy:

"Oh give thanks unto (the Lord); for he is good; for his lovingkindness endureth for ever." - Psalm 107:1

It is the banner over her life.

For Eleanor Grace Lockhart was never meant to wither in a windowless office. She was meant for the garden. Meant for fragrance and faith. Meant to craft beauty from earth and prayer.

And she is blooming still.

The Blue that Wasn't Water
By an author who remembers how summer once felt

They hadn't expected the quiet.

That was the first thing they noticed, stepping out of the removal van into the stillness of the village. After years of city life - sirens, buses, shouting, the constant cacophony - they stood in their new front garden blinking, as if the silence itself was something loud and unfamiliar.

Henry, the older of the two, was sixteen. Kenelm was fourteen, though everyone mistook them for twins, their features drawn from the same gentle mould, their dark hair curling in the same stubborn way. Both stood, nonplussed, on the warm flagstones, a little stunned by the sudden emptiness of noise.

But then, as their ears adjusted, other sounds began to emerge: a robin's chatter from the hedge, the distant bleat of sheep, the breeze sighing through an old ash tree at the end of the garden. Not silence, then, just a different kind of music.

Above them, a red kite wheeled in the clear sky, its wings catching the sunlight as it called out in a high, mewing cry.

"Did you know it would be like this?" Kenelm asked.

Henry shook his head slowly. "Not this. I thought it'd be quieter than London, yes. But this... this is something else."

They'd moved to a village nestled in the Chilterns Area of Outstanding Natural Beauty, a place their mother had spoken of as "God's own garden" when she came back from viewing the house. It hadn't made much sense to them then. It did now.

That evening, their mother pointed out the narrow road that led from the edge of their little cul-de-sac to the Catholic church - only three minutes away on foot. They could go any time, she said. Jesus was always there, waiting, in the stillness of the tabernacle.

Something about that rooted itself in their minds. A church just down the road. No buses, no traffic, just a few steps and they were in the presence of God. This felt so awe-inspiring and reassuring, not to mention convenient. A steady anchor in a world that was suddenly quiet and new.

The church itself was simple: modern, brick-built, with light flooding in through tall windows and the scent of wood polish rather than incense. But it was beautiful in its own way. There was nothing showy, nothing grand. Just space. Peace. Presence.

But it was the following morning that the real magic began.

They'd wandered to the end of their street, past the post box and the overgrown cottage with a missing shutter, where a kissing gate opened onto a barely visible path. Beyond it, a hedgerow arched overhead like a secret entrance to another world. And when they pushed through - boots brushing grass, brambles tugging at their sleeves - they entered it.

The path widened. The world opened.

Before them lay fields as wide and golden as dreams, dotted with dandelions, poppies and butterflies. Trees lined the ridges like watchmen, and the sky, impossibly blue for England, seemed to stretch into forever.

Kenelm let out a low whistle.

"Are you sure this isn't someone's land?" he asked.

Henry grinned. "It's all someone's land. But look, there's a footpath sign. It's allowed."

The countryside unfolded like a story they'd never read before. They followed the winding trail through fields buzzing with bees and thick with the warm scent of grass and wild herbs. They found an old wooden stile with initials carved deep into its beam, and a stream trickling silver between pebbled banks. Birds flitted overhead - swallows, goldfinches, something blue they couldn't name - and butterflies like shards of sunlight danced among the hedges.

And then they saw it.

At first, it looked like water. A shimmer of soft blue across the far side of the field, rippling faintly in the breeze.

"It's a lake," Kenelm said, stepping forward. But Henry narrowed his eyes.

"Wait… not a lake. Look closer."

They crossed the field in slow wonder until they stood at its edge.

Not water. Flowers. A sea of them. *Baby blue eyes* - nemophila - spread in a quiet riot of colour, thousands upon thousands swaying together like something from a painter's dream. The boys stood wordless for a long time.

"I didn't know flowers could do this," Kenelm said softly.

Henry bent to touch one, careful not to crush it. "I didn't know the world could."

They didn't speak for a while, not really needing to. Something sacred hung in the air - an unspoken awe. Later, as they walked home through glistening fields of gold wheat and back through the hedgerow path, they talked about their future. Not in concrete plans, but hopes. Possibilities. They spoke of becoming good men, of doing something worthwhile, of finding joy and love and keeping close to God.

And they realised something else, too. Something quiet and important.

These days in the sun, these paths through fields and flowers and light - they were drawing the two of them closer. Each step taken in wonder became another thread in the bond between them. The more beauty they discovered, the more they felt it was being shared between them. As though their souls, walking side by side, were catching fire from the same flame.

"I'd like to stay here," Kenelm said.

"Me too," said Henry. "Feels like it's brushed with Heaven."

Each day that followed in that soft-bright August unfolded with quiet miracles. They woke early and went to Mass, the quiet little church glowing in morning light. They knelt together, side by side and whispered prayers for the day ahead.

Then they wandered - exploring further each time. They found a glade where deer had slept, still warm to the touch. They saw dragonflies darting like glass through sunlight and walked beneath oaks so old their bark seemed etched with scripture. And always, above them, the red kites soared.

There were no big events. No dramas. Just the still, constant presence of something larger than themselves. They were no longer just brothers. They were fellow pilgrims, walking the same quiet road into the heart of God.

One evening, just before the sun dipped behind the hills, they stood on the highest field, where the whole landscape unfolded like a painted scroll. Everything was golden - the sky, the fields, even their own faces in the light.

Kenelm turned to Henry and said, "Whatever we do. Whatever life brings… let's stick together."

Henry didn't hesitate. "Yes," he said. "Always."

The wind stirred the wheat. The sky glowed deeper gold. And in that moment, in the middle of nowhere, the two boys - brothers, dreamers, children of God - knew what grace felt like.

Not loud. Not complicated.

Just joy. Just wonder.
Just love, poured out over everything, like light.

The Whiffleton Hall Capers

Chapter One: In Which Gussie Buys a Pile of Rubble

When Augustus Bembridge-Paddleton first clapped eyes on Whiffleton Hall, he described it as "a hidden gem of the Georgian period". Others, such as the estate agent, called it "a fixer-upper with character". His wife, Clarissa, upon first seeing it, called it "a lawsuit waiting to happen".

Located on the sunny south coast of the Isle of Wroth - a largely overlooked island situated somewhere between the Isle of Wight and the mainland - Whiffleton Hall had stood for three centuries, with the dogged determination of a true Islander. The roof was only partly attached, the west wing leaned in a way that suggested it had given up trying, and the garden was under the misapprehension it was a jungle.

"Look at the bones, old girl," Gussie said proudly as a chunk of masonry fell behind him. "They don't build them like this anymore!"

"They wouldn't *dare*," Clarissa muttered.

Chapter Two: A Man for All Ceilings

Renovations began the way most disasters do: with optimism and scaffolding. Enter Monty Spreebuckle, a man with the kind of smile that made women swoon and accountants weep. He introduced himself with a flourish and an accent that had been to several public schools and survived them all.

"I specialise in the *sympathetic* restoration of ancestral

estates," he declared.

Clarissa narrowed her eyes. "Sympathetic, as in... you feel sorry for them?"

Monty smiled. "Deeply."

Within a fortnight, Monty had convinced Gussie to commission a folly, three orangeries, and a water feature that required plumbing permits from the 18th century.

Chapter Three: The Great Wall Collapse and Other Amusements

It was during an impromptu drinks gathering that the *entire* north wall of the dining room decided to migrate southward. Twinge, who had just returned with the sherry, took it rather stoically.

"Shall I serve it in the billiards room, sir? The ceiling's still attached there."

The guests, mostly members of the local Historical Society and one confused French tourist, applauded politely. Lord Bletchley-Bloater, four gins in, declared it a "capital bit of renovation" and proposed a toast "to progress!"

Clarissa, on the other hand, took to writing increasingly sharp letters to the Isle of Wroth Borough Council (IWBC), none of which were answered except by an enthusiastic intern who suggested turning the Hall into an escape room.

Chapter Four: Monty's Scheme

Comes Crumbling Down

It was Gussie's beloved dog, Pickles, who finally uncovered Monty Spreebuckle's true identity - literally - by digging up a briefcase full of forged documents under the ornamental duck pond.

A dramatic confrontation ensued in the partially restored library. Monty tried to flee via the servants' stair, only to be thwarted by Twinge, who had been polishing the bannister with such fervour that Monty slid all the way back down into a flowerpot.

"I believe, sir," Twinge said with faint satisfaction, "that he's quite finished consulting."

Chapter Five: Restoration, Reputations and Other Risky Endeavours

With Monty sent packing, the Bembridge-Paddletons began the restoration anew - this time with local craftsmen, real architects, and slightly less delusion. Gussie took to writing a memoir about their experience called *"Folly and Fortune: My Life with Damp."*

Whiffleton Hall was eventually restored enough to host a charity garden fête, during which only one gazebo collapsed and nobody was bitten by anything worse than a wasp.

Lord Bletchley-Bloater, now a regular fixture in their drawing room, toasted them again.

"You know, I always said this place had potential," he beamed.

Clarissa smiled through gritted teeth. "Yes. And now it only leaks in *two* rooms."

As Gussie looked out over the crumbling balustrade of the east terrace, he turned to Clarissa with a beatific grin.

"Well, darling, I daresay we've made it our own."

Clarissa gazed at the slightly crooked chimney, the ivy-covered gargoyles and the smoke rising from the kitchen in what might have been a fire.

"Yes," she said. "It's *definitely* ours. Nobody else would want it."

Chapter Six: In Which an Engine Escapes, a Lagonda Takes Flight, and Someone Ends Up in the Pond

It was a fine summer morning at Whiffleton Hall, by local standards, and preparations were underway for the Annual Upper Wroth Heritage Hoorah, a village event of such dazzling mediocrity that it had, over time, become oddly beloved. This year, due to some frightful administrative error (likely involving sherry and a rotary phone), Whiffleton Hall had been chosen to host it.

Clarissa was in the south garden arguing with a man named Clifford, about bunting tension. Gussie was in the drive trying to start his 1930 Lagonda 2-Litre with a spanner, an absinthe spoon and a prayer.

"Clarissa!" he called. "I think it's purring!"

"It's *smoking*," she called back.

"Even better!"

Meanwhile, Monty Spreebuckle, freshly rebranded as "Consultant Director of Heritage Festivities", stood upon a tea crate holding a megaphone and wearing a straw boater three sizes too large.

"Ladies and gentlemen," he bellowed to a collection of pensioners, a ferret on a lead, and two glum vicars. "Behold! The marvels of our national past!"

At which point, a steam traction engine named *Breakspear Two* let out a hiss like a startled goose and lurched forward.

"Should it be moving?" asked someone.

"It's stationary," said Monty. "Symbolically."

"No, I mean it's heading for the gazebo."

Clarissa turned. "*GUSSIE!*"

Gussie, hearing his name (and assuming someone wanted a ride in the Lagonda), turned the key. With a throaty growl, the car burst into life, performed what could only be described as a wheelspin of joy, and shot directly onto the lawn.

"View halloooo!" Gussie cried, for no discernible reason, as the car bounded over a flower bed, clipped a sundial, and continued across the grass with single-minded idiocy, toward the ornamental pond.

A duck quacked in alarm.

Then the Lagonda sailed magnificently into the pond like a jazz-era swan dive.

Splash.

From the driver's seat emerged Gussie, waterlogged and faintly euphoric.

"Clarissa," he said, wading ashore, "I believe we've found the smugglers' tunnel entrance."

"No, dear," she sighed. "You've found the old koi pond."

Meanwhile, at the Carousel…

As if drawn by chaos, the Victorian carousel - on loan from a man named Trevor whose main qualification was a moustache and the phrase *"It'll hold"* - began spinning slowly of its own accord. No one was on it. The organ began playing a slightly haunted rendition of "Rule, Britannia".

Monty, seeing a PR opportunity, leapt aboard.

"Observe, the timeless joy of the steam fair!" he cried, striking a pose on a wooden giraffe.

"Monty," called Clarissa, "is it supposed to be *that fast?*"

"It's atmospheric!"

"It's doing thirty!"

Around it spun - Monty, the giraffe, a large ceramic pig, and a confused child in a sailor suit who had somehow climbed aboard mid-spin and was now holding on like a naval cadet in a hurricane.

The carousel, emboldened by momentum and hubris, broke free of its wheel chocks, rolled gently downhill, and collided with the tea tent, leaving a trail of Victoria sponge and broken deck chairs in its wake. Luckily, no one was hurt.

As for the runaway traction engine, Miss Fenella Throstle had heroically intervened - leaping aboard at the last possible moment and steering it away with surprising authority. They were last seen crossing the bridge to the Isle of Wight at considerable speed. The gazebo was saved.

Fenella has not been seen since, though her postcard from Cowes was cheerful.

Aftermath

Twinge, brushing sponge from his lapels, surveyed the ruins of the fête.

"Well, sir," he said, addressing Gussie, who was drying his socks on the lawn, "I'd say that went slightly better than last year."

Gussie beamed. "You really think so?"

"Indeed. No one caught fire this time."

Clarissa, taking it all in, turned to Monty - who was now eating trifle from a bent serving tray.

"You," she said, "are banned from clipboards, tents, or anything powered by steam."

Monty saluted. "Understood. Might I interest you in an Edwardian penny-farthing joust for the autumn fête?"

"*Out.*"

Chapter Seven: In Which Whiffleton Goes Full Regency and the Bishop Reappears by Accident

It began, as so many things at Whiffleton Hall did, with a costume hire invoice that Gussie had signed without reading.

"A Regency Weekend!" he proclaimed, waving a tricorn hat with dangerous enthusiasm. "Authentic dancing, rustic amusements, light duelling!"

"You've never duelled anyone," said Clarissa.

"Not officially," Gussie replied. "But I *once* brandished a focaccia at a travel agent in Verona, as you well know."

The plan, such as it was, involved transforming the estate into a vision of Georgian splendour: croquet on the lawn, syllabub in the conservatory, and at least three minor footmen in periwigs collapsing from heat exhaustion.

Clarissa watched a man in a cravat wrestle a collapsing marquee and sighed.

"This is either going to bankrupt us," she said, "or be a triumph that bankrupts us."

Enter the Guests (and the Muddle Begins)

The guests began arriving just after lunch - members of local societies with names like *The Hampshire Enthusiasts of Breeches*, *Janeites Anonymous* and *The Round Table of Historical Reenactment and Trifle Appreciation*.

Monty, naturally, had appointed himself Master of Ceremonies and was circulating in an outfit that could only be described as "Dandy Highwayman meets sofa upholstery".

Clarissa took one look. "You're wearing curtains."

"I *am* the moodboard," he replied grandly.

At Gussie's instruction, Twinge had prepared the cellar as a "Brandy Parlour Experience", which mostly involved dim lighting, too many candles, and a stuffed pheasant named Napoleon.

It was somewhere between preparations for the mock duel (foam swords, no bruising) and the Quadrille Reenactment Disaster of 3:15pm that the matter of the *priest hole* came up.

Chapter Seven (continued): In Which the Bishop Reappears, Quite Cheerfully, from Behind the Wainscot

It was just after Lord Bletchley-Bloater accidentally concussed a vicar with a decorative epergne (Regency-themed, highly impractical) that the shout rang out from the library:

"There's a hole behind the wainscot!"

Everyone paused. Even the hurdy-gurdy player fell momentarily silent, though this may have been due to heatstroke or gin.

Clarissa arrived on the scene to find Mr Peebles of the Trifle Appreciation Society waving a candelabra at a dislodged panel.

"Felt a draught behind the Byron volumes," he explained. "And possibly heard Gregorian chanting."

"More likely Twinge humming," Clarissa said, peering into the gloom.

The space revealed was narrow, dusty and surprisingly vertical.

"A priest hole!" Monty gasped, appearing in full sash and riding boots. "Clarissa, Gussie, you're saved!"

"We *are* Catholic," Clarissa muttered, "but that's not usually how we advertise the Hall."

"No," said Gussie, catching on, eyes gleaming, "but think of the brochure! *Whiffleton Hall: Recusant Secrets!* Guided tours! Heritage grants! Pilgrims in stout footwear!"

Clarissa narrowed her eyes. "You think a priest hole is going to save us?"

"I think," said Gussie, "that a priest hole, a velvet rope, and a gift shop might just buy us a new roof."

At that moment, a firm and familiar voice echoed from within the panelling.

"Hullo? Is that the billiards room?"

Then, with the practised dignity of a man accustomed to unusual exits, The Most Reverend Cyril Fortescue-Dunstable (*The Fort*, as he was known to his fellow *Old Eggs* from Upforth Edge), Bishop Emeritus of the Catholic Diocese of Greater Gosport, stepped out of the priest hole and into polite society.

He was freshly shaven, mildly pink-cheeked and radiating the serene good health of a man who had recently been delivered honeycomb doughnuts and a local crab pasty.

"Bishop Cyril!" Monty cried, delighted. "We thought you'd gone back to Gosport!"

"I attempted to," said the Bishop cheerfully, brushing a speck of plaster from his sleeve. "Then I took a wrong turning after breakfast. I was admiring the Engleheart miniatures, stepped back to contemplate them *en masse* - too far back, as you may observe - and the panel clicked shut. Thought I'd wait until someone came looking. Didn't expect a full Regency weekend in the interim."

Clarissa blinked. "You've been in there *this whole time?*"

"Oh yes, since Tuesday. Quite comfortable, really. One of your volunteers passed me a sandwich on Thursday. Roast beef. Excellent crust."

"You should've shouted!"

"I *did* shout," explained the Bishop, placidly. "But the jazz quartet in the parlour were doing Mary Lou Williams' *Night*

Life and rather drowned me out."

"I found," he continued, "a copy of *Country Life* from 1996 and rationed a travel-sized Madeira cake from my coat pocket. So, it was all quite civilised, really."

"Remarkable man," Lord Bletchley-Bloater said, to no one in particular. "Would've made a first-rate spy."

"I *was* once mistaken for a French count in Palermo," the Bishop admitted. "But that's a story for the port."

Monty, naturally, had already produced a decanter and three glasses from somewhere inside his Regency costume.

"To *The Fort!*" Gussie declared, raising his glass to toast the Bishop. "Survivor of cake, panelling and a miniatures misadventure."

"*The Fort!*" came the chorus, just as Jenkins, looking somewhat resigned, appeared with the news that the duck - *that* duck, the one whose exploits were practically legendary around the estate - had once again taken up residence in the scullery and was embarking on yet another of its notorious campaigns, this time targeting a guest's bonnet.

Leaving duck-related business to Gussie, Clarissa's eyes locked onto the decanter in Monty's hands, then flicked to his guilty expression.

"Monty," she said, voice like ice, "is that *my* port?"

Monty froze, glass halfway to his lips. "I... uh..."

"*Out.*"

"I wasn't -"

"***Out.***"

With a sigh, Monty straightened and made a hasty exit, muttering something about soufflés and 'future invitations'.

"Good riddance," Clarissa muttered, turning back to the group. "Now, where were we?"

"Monty's always one step away from the door, isn't he?" said Gussie. "I'm sure we'll be seeing him again soon."

Chapter Eight: In Which Foam Swords Fly and Cravats Bend

The rest of the evening progressed in its usual haywire manner. The guests, once fully recovered from the Quadrille Reenactment Disaster of 3:15pm (which had involved two sprained ankles, three misplaced hatpins, and a large amount of trifle on the floor), returned to their socialising with renewed vigour.

Lord Binstead, his cravat now dangerously askew, had been pronounced the winner of the mock duel after he'd tripped over a decorative chair and landed on his opponent, thus ensuring an entirely unexpected victory. No one had been quite sure how to tally it up, but the foam swords had certainly been put to good use. A round of applause followed, not for the duel itself, but for the impressive way in which Lord Binstead had maintained his dignity despite being set upon by a particularly feisty indoor rose bush.

The Bishop settled himself by a dish of delicate almond cakes, tucking in with the vigour of a man who had spent the past few days in a cupboard. Just as he finished his third, a lady in a towering bonnet approached him, asking, deferentially, "Your Grace, might you bless my wig?"

Monty, who had been unambiguously removed after the port incident, had somehow reappeared, unchanged in outfit and outlook, now detailing ideas involving a swan-shaped fountain and an amateur circus to bolster visitor numbers. Clarissa mused, not for the first time, on the lower ha-ha: dry this time of year, reasonably deep, and more than capable of discouraging repeat Monty appearances.

But, all in all, the evening was a resounding success - or at least, a *somewhat* successful disaster. Gussie could already see the brochure material forming in his mind: *Whiffleton Hall - House of Secrets: Heroes, Hidden Heritage and Hair's-Breadth Escapes!*

As the final waltz of the evening came to a rather shaky close (no one, it turned out, had ever properly learned how to perform the *Pantomime Minuet*), Clarissa surveyed the room with a calm, almost serene satisfaction.

"See?" she said, turning to Gussie. "This is exactly what I told you. A triumph that bankrupts us."

And with that, they retired to the library, leaving the guests to debate whether the duck's insurrection was a sign of deeper unrest or merely an exceptionally determined fowl.

Where the Heather Meets the Sky

The train had left her at Hope, and from there she had walked. The old footpaths were still there, winding their way through sheep-grazed fields and low dry-stone walls, familiar as breathing. With her rucksack on her back and the rhythm of her boots on earth, she passed under ash trees and over stiles, slowly ascending into the hills that had once been her whole world.

Anna had not returned to the Peak District in decades - not properly, not with time in her pocket and no hurry to be anywhere else. Now, in her mid-forties, life had thinned itself down to essentials. She had left the city behind: its meetings, its trains, its unrelenting buzz. And she had come here, to the north-eastern edges of the Peaks, not merely to rest, but to remember. To listen.

Nestled between a shoulder of hill and a brook that gurgled like soft laughter, the cottage appeared as if summoned. A tangle of late-summer roses clambered over its stone walls, and pale green shutters framed small windows that looked out across the valley. The path to the door was edged with thyme and mint, their scent rising as her boots disturbed the leaves. A wooden bench, worn smooth by time and weather, sat in the shade of an old rowan tree, its red berries beginning to blush.

Inside, the rooms were cool and low-beamed, with flagstone floors and handwoven rugs. A wood-burning stove stood in the hearth, and shelves held pottery mugs, beeswax candles, and old books with broken spines. The kettle sang softly on the hob. Anna placed her satchel down, unwrapped her rosary from its linen pouch, and sat in the armchair by the small mullioned window, gazing out across the heather.

The next morning, she woke early, dressed in layers, and set off with a flask of tea, and a slice of flapjack in her pocket. The path led upwards, following the old sheep tracks past moss-slicked boulders and long grass that swayed in the breeze. The air was so fresh, untouched and clean, that she felt every breath. Birds wheeled and darted above: goldfinches, starlings, the whispery flight of a barn owl returning to its roost.

To her right, Ladybower Reservoir shimmered in the early light, its long arms reaching through the valley like a mirror to the sky. Mist curled over the surface, and the surrounding hills stood proud and purple with heather, their rocky outcrops softened by time and wind. Every step she took landed on springy turf or the broad backs of ancient gritstone, each one releasing the scent of earth and wild thyme.

She paused often - not from tiredness, but wonder. Butterflies danced between clumps of harebell and bracken. Skylarks lifted their hymn into the vast blue overhead. It was a place made not merely for walking, but for praise. And though she spoke no words aloud, Anna's every breath felt like prayer.

As she reached a rise in the land above Hathersage, the landscape stretched wide and wild before her. She sat down on a sun-warmed rock and unscrewed her thermos flask. In the far distance, the faint bells of a village church carried on the breeze. She closed her eyes and was eight years old again… cheeks pink from snow, stomping up the lane in wellington boots, her fingers curled around her mother's hand. In those days, winter meant roads impassable, school cancelled, and a nail-biting drive into Hillsborough for Mass. She could still feel the candle-warmed hush of Sacred Heart, the scent of wax and pine, her father's voice low in prayer beside her.

That memory wrapped itself around her now, gentle and whole. The years between then and now fell quiet. She had left the hills behind once, believing that purpose lay in noise and striving. But now, she saw clearly: peace was not something to earn. It was something to return to.

She had come back not just to walk, or to rest, but to listen for the voice she had lost in the noise. And in this high, open place, that voice came: not loud, not dramatic. Just a stillness. A knowing.

Anna took out her rosary and let the beads slip through her fingers. The prayers came slowly, like water finding its course after a long drought. She did not rush. God was here… in the heather, the wind, the hush of the valley. In her.

She stayed on the ridge until the light turned gold and the shadows lengthened. Then she followed the path home, the stone cottage waiting like a lamp in the dusk.

That evening, seated once more by the window, a blanket round her shoulders, she opened her journal and wrote just one sentence: *I want to live here.*

No car. No hurry. No ladder to climb. Just a cottage in the middle of nowhere, a daily walk to Mass in Hathersage, a garden full of bees, and time enough to pray each hour like it mattered.

She would return for good.

And there, in the quiet cleft of the hills, where the heather meets the sky, she would begin again. Not alone, but with God.

Lavender Field of Grace

The sun, still soft from its early rise, bathed the rolling hills of the Northumberland countryside in a golden light that washed over the heathered moors and wind-brushed meadows like liquid gold. In the distance, the wild, rounded slopes of the Cheviot Hills, softened by the haze of summer, glowed a gentle amber. On the edge of a small village, tucked away behind dry stone walls and ivy-covered cottages, was a plot of land that had once been abandoned, but was now being brought to life with purpose and love. Here, the air smelled of dew-kissed earth, lavender and the promise of a new beginning.

Lydia stood at the gate of the farm, watching her son, Aidan, crouch low in the grass, his fingers brushing the leaves of the young lavender plants they had set in the earth only weeks before. His movements were precise, deliberate, as though he were conversing with the plants in a language only he understood. Aidan was twenty-two, but in many ways, he had always seemed older. His mind worked in its own way, his thoughts ordered and quiet, and he found peace in patterns, whether it was the rhythm of his favourite clock, the steady pulse of rain against the windows or the repetitive task of tending to the lavender.

Aidan had been diagnosed with autism at an early age and, though it was often a struggle to communicate with him, Lydia had always noticed there was something special and extraordinary within him. He brought her a heartfelt joy, a sense of wonder that softened even the hardest days. He was her blessing, her boy, her glimpse of Heaven on Earth. It had been her faith that had guided her through the darkest of days, but it was her love for Aidan that made her heart keep choosing hope, that told her to hold on, to never give up, to trust in God's plan for them both.

Two years ago, after the loss of her husband to a sudden illness, Lydia had felt adrift. The house felt too large, the silence too loud. But when Aidan showed an unusual interest in the large, unused patch of land behind their cottage, something shifted inside her. The idea of starting a lavender farm wasn't one that made immediate sense to anyone else: how could she manage it on her own, especially when Aidan struggled with change, with routine, with people? Aidan didn't speak - not in words - but there was a stillness in his eyes when he gazed at the field and, in her heart, Lydia knew this was something they were meant to do together.

They had started small. A few rows of lavender, then a few more. Lydia worked tirelessly, learning everything she could about the delicate plants. Aidan, on the other hand, took to it with quiet devotion. He had always preferred solitary work, and this was perfect for him: sowing, watering, pruning. Every morning, Lydia would rise with the sun, and they would spend hours in their ever-increasing garden.

Though Aidan rarely spoke, Lydia understood him in a way she never had before. In the scent of lavender, she saw him coming to life in ways words could never express. He was calm. He was present. He was connected. As the lavender grew tall and strong, so did their bond. And in each flower that bloomed, Lydia saw the love of God - a love that was patient, enduring, and always blooming, even in the midst of trials.

The farm slowly began to flourish, and with it, so did their lives. Aidan's behaviour began to stabilise, and Lydia saw him in moments of clarity she had never experienced before. He began to bring small bouquets of lavender to her, his fingers expertly tying them with twine.

One evening, as they sat on the back porch overlooking the fields, Aidan turned to her with a rare, quiet smile. "Mum," he said, his voice soft, but clear. "Lavender means 'hope.'"

Lydia's breath caught in her throat. The words hung in the air like a prayer answered. "Yes, darling," she replied, her heart swelling. "Lavender means hope."

It had taken years of faith, of perseverance, of understanding that God's timing was perfect, but here they were, on a lavender farm, surrounded by purple blooms and the soft buzzing of bees, their hearts intertwined with the beauty of creation. Lydia knew now, more than ever, that her purpose was not just to care for Aidan, but to nurture the growth of all that was good and holy in their lives.

As the sun set behind the lavender field, casting long shadows on the ground, the soft light of dusk turned the Cheviot Hills into a silhouette of quiet majesty. The colours of the evening sky, painted in hues of purple and pink, seemed to whisper a promise of peace. Lydia breathed a prayer of gratitude. "Thank you, Lord, for giving us this place. For Aidan. For teaching me to trust in You, even when the way was uncertain."

And in that moment, she knew, deep in her soul, that God's plan for them was unfolding just as it was meant to. The lavender farm was more than just a dream realised. It was a testimony of grace - of faith, of love, of patience. It was a symbol of the new beginning they had found together, one where they could grow, flourish, and, with God's help, heal.

The lavender field swayed gently in the breeze, and Lydia smiled as she watched Aidan, his face lifted to the sky, his heart at peace.

It was a good life. It was a blessed life.
And it was just the beginning.

Printed in Dunstable, United Kingdom

67713176R00109